OXFORD
GCSE Maths for OCR

SPECIFICATION A

Revision Guide

Steve Cavill
Geoff Gibb
Jayne Kranat
Neil Tully

OCR — RECOGNISING ACHIEVEMENT
OXFORD UNIVERSITY PRESS
Official Publisher Partnership

Great Clarendon Street, Oxford OX2 6DP

Oxford University Press is a department of the University of Oxford.

It furthers the University's objective of excellence in research, scholarship, and education by publishing worldwide in

Oxford   New York

Auckland Cape Town Dar es Salaam Hong Kong Karachi
Kuala Lumpur Madrid Melbourne Mexico City Nairobi
New Delhi Shanghai Taipei Toronto

With offices in

Argentina Austria Brazil Chile Czech Republic France Greece
Guatemala Hungary Italy Japan Poland Portugal Singapore
South Korea Switzerland Thailand Turkey Ukraine Vietnam

© Oxford University Press

The moral rights of the authors have been asserted

Database right Oxford University Press (maker)

First published 2011

All rights reserved. No part of this publication may be reproduced, stored in a retrieval system, or transmitted, in any form or by any means, without the prior permission in writing of Oxford University Press, or as expressly permitted by law, or under terms agreed with the appropriate reprographics rights organization. Enquiries concerning reproduction outside the scope of the above should be sent to the Rights Department, Oxford University Press, at the address above

You must not circulate this book in any other binding or cover and you must impose this same condition on any acquirer

British Library Cataloguing in Publication Data

Data available

ISBN: 978-0-19-912804-4
10 9 8 7 6 5 4 3

Printed in Great Britain by Bell and Bain Ltd, Glasgow

We are grateful to the following for permission to reproduce copyright material:

Front cover: Tatiana53/Shutterstock; Oscar E. Gutierrez/iStock; Krivoy Rog/iStock; nel4/iStock

Paper used in the production of this book is a natural, recyclable product made from wood grown in sustainable forests. The manufacturing process conforms to the environmental regulations to the country of origin.

About this book

Produced in partnership with OCR, this revision guide contains all the material you need to help you prepare for your Foundation tier examinations in OCR's GCSE in Mathematics A (J562). Written by senior examiners and OCR teachers, the book provides:

- Key points, worked examples and exercises for each topic to help you fully consolidate the learning objectives
- Sample papers for valuable exam practice including the new assessment objectives
- A free CD-ROM containing all pages in PDF format for flexible learning, as well as full solutions and mark schemes for the sample papers

Contents

UNIT A

AN1	Arithmetic with integers	2
AN2	Arithmetic with decimals	4
AN3	Rounding and approximation	6
AN4	Factors, multiples and primes	8
AN5	Calculator skills	10
AN6	Order of operations	12
AN7	Basic ratio	14
AN8	Using ratio	16
AA1	Symbols	18
AA2	Coordinates	20
AA3	Formulae	22
AA4	Sequences	24
AA5	Equations	26
AA6	Brackets	28
AG1	Measures and scales	30
AG2	Constructions	32
AG3	Loci	34
AG4	Scale drawing	36
AG5	Maps and bearings	38
AG6	Pythagoras' theorem	40
AS1	Collecting and handling data	42
AS2	Averages and range	44
AS3	Finding averages from tables	46
AS4	Pie charts and bar charts	48
AS5	Histograms and frequency polygons	50

UNIT B

BN1	Arithmetic with integers and decimals	52
BN2	Estimating and checking decimal calculations	54
BN3	Terminating and recurring decimals	56
BN4	Fractions and decimals	58
BN5	Calculating with fractions	60
BN6	Percentages, fractions and decimals	62
BN7	Squares and cubes	64
BN8	Indices and index laws	66
BA1	Straight-line graphs	68
BA2	Real-life linear functions	70
BA3	Inequalities	72
BG1	Basic geometry	74
BG2	Polygons and quadrilaterals	76
BG3	Translations	78
BG4	Symmetry, reflection and rotation	80
BG5	Combining transformations	82
BG6	Congruence and similarity	84
BG7	Enlargements	86
BG8	The language of circles	88
BS1	Scatter graphs	90
BS2	Time series	92

UNIT C

CN1	Calculating with fractions and rounding	94
CN2	Calculator skills and formulae	96
CN3	Percentage problems	98
CN4	Bounds of measurement	100
CN5	Proportion	101
CN6	Compound measures	102
CA1	3D coordinates	104
CA2	Trial and improvement	105
CA3	Graphs from real life	106
CA4	Graphs of quadratic functions	107
CG1	Perimeter and area of basic shapes	108
CG2	Circumference and area of circles	110
CG3	Area of parallelograms and trapeziums	112
CG4	Plans, elevations and nets	114
CG5	Surface area and volume	116
CG6	Length, area and volume scale	118
CS1	Theoretical probability	120
CS2	Mutually exclusive events	122
CS3	Listing outcomes	124
CS4	Experiments and relative frequency	126

GCSE formulae	128
Practice paper A	129
Practice paper B	134
Practice paper C	139
Answers	146

Arithmetic with integers

AN1

You can **add** and **subtract** integers by counting **moves** along a number line.
To work out 6 – 8 – 2, start at 6, count back 8 moves (to –2) and then 2 more to –4.

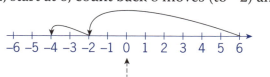

> –4 is 10 smaller than 6.
> Count the moves from –4 to 6.
> You make 10 moves.

- Negative numbers are smaller than 0 | Positive numbers are larger than 0

Addition, subtraction, multiplication and division are all mathematical operations. You will hear different words for mathematical operations. Here are some examples.

Operation	Key word
Add	Total, altogether, sum
Subtract	Difference between, minus
Multiply	Lots of, times, product
Divide	Share, how many in…

EXAMINER'S TIP

Read the question carefully and look for the key words.
Think about the answer. If it is not sensible, have you used the right operation?

EXAMPLE

Sue, Liam and Jack share the cost of a meal equally.
The meal costs £24.60.
How much do they each pay?

£24.60 ÷ 3 = £8.20

> Your calculator shows 8.2
> Remember to put in the 0 and £ sign.

When you **multiply** or **divide** a number by 10, 100, 1000, … the digits do not change, only the number of zeros.

a 90 × 100 = 9000

		9	0
9	0	0	0

b 3 ÷ 10 = 0.3

3	.	0
0	.	3

Learn the rules for multiplying and dividing with **directed** (negative and positive) **numbers**.

× or ÷	–	+
–	+	–
+	–	+

Examples
a 2 × –3 = –6
b –15 ÷ –3 = 5
c 15 × –2 ÷ 5 = –6

EXAMINER'S TIP

As a check, count the number of minus signs in the sum.
If this is even, the answer is +
If it is odd, the answer is –
a only 1 minus (odd) answer –
b 2 minuses (even) answer +
c only 1 minus (odd) answer –

EXAMPLE

The sum of three integers is 5. Two of the integers are negative.
Write two different sets of integers that obey these rules.

14, –3 and –6   **and**   20, –12 and –3

> There are many different possible answers.

Exercise AN1

LOW

1. Work these out   a $12 \div -6$ b $-32 \times 2 \times -2$ c $-21 - 8$ d $-21 + 8$

2. Draw a number line from -30 to -10. Use your number line to explain why
   a the answer to question **1c** is smaller than -21
   b the answer to question **1d** is larger than -21.

3. Explain how you know these answers are wrong just by looking at them.
   a $123 \times -2 = 246$ b $25 \div -5 = 5$ c $-8 \times -5 \times -2 = 80$ d $10 \times -2 = 20$

4. Finn buys 24 large loaves to make sandwiches. Each loaf has 18 slices, including the end crusts, which he cannot use. He needs 2 slices to make a sandwich. How many sandwiches can he make?

5. Carla flies from London to Rome at Christmas. The temperature in Rome is 14 °C and the temperature in London is -5 °C. How much hotter is Rome than London?

6. Harry sees this advert.
   a How much money does he save if he buys 3 Choc Stars?
   b Because they melt quickly he sells one to Ali for 95p and one to Rita for 95p. How much has his Choc Star cost him?

Choc Star
£1.23 each or 3 for £2.80

7. This table shows the average heights, in mm, of boys and girls in the UK.
   a How many mm do boys grow, on average, between the ages of 11 years and 18 years?
   b How many mm does the average boy grow in height in 1 year?
   c How many mm does the average girl grow in height in 1 year?
   d Explain what your answers tell you and why this might not be the whole story.

	Height	
Age	Girls	Boys
11	1440	1430
12	1500	1490
13	1550	1550
14	1590	1630
15	1610	1690
16	1620	1730
17	1620	1750
18	1620	1760

8. Here is a puzzle.
   Three negative integers have a sum of -10.
   The largest integer is 3 more than the smallest one.
   When the integers are multiplied together the answer is -30.
   What are the three integers?

9. There are 12 inches in a foot and 3 feet in a yard.
   The distance round a circle is roughly three times the distance across it.
   a How many inches is it round the centre circle of a football field if the distance across the circle is 20 yards?
   b What is this distance in feet?

Arithmetic with integers

Arithmetic with decimals

AN2

You can use the same rules for decimals as you do for integers.
- When you **multiply** a decimal number, move the digits **left** the same number of columns as there are **zeros** in the multiplier.

When you **divide** a decimal number, move the digits **right** the same number of columns as there are zeros in the divider.

EXAMPLE

Work out
- a 23×1000
- b 2.9×100
- c $41 \div 100$
- d $0.3 \div 10$
- e $13.26 \div 100$
- f $145\,269 \times 10\,000\,000$

a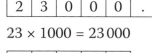
$23 \times 1000 = 23\,000$

b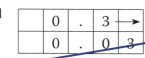
$2.9 \times 100 = 290$

c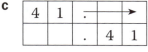
$41 \div 100 = 0.41$

d
| | 0 | . | 3 | → |
| | 0 | . | 0 | 3 |

$0.3 \div 10 = 0.03$

e 0.1326

f $1\,452\,690\,000\,000$

> **EXAMINER'S TIP**
> There is an invisible decimal point at the end of every whole number. Use zeros to fill columns between a digit and the decimal point.

> In part **a** write 0 in front of the decimal point to show the point clearly.

> **EXAMINER'S TIP**
> Your calculator will say 1.45269×10^{12}. It is easier just to move the digits 7 places (because there are 7 zeros in 10 million).

You can multiply or divide by a positive number **between 0 and 1**.

×	The answer is smaller than the original number.	$25 \times 0.5 = 12.5$
÷	The answer is larger than the original number.	$25 \div 0.5 = 50$

25 halves make 12.5

There are 50 halves in 25

EXAMPLE

Steve pays 15.27p a unit for his electricity. He uses 418 units. What is his bill, in pounds?

$15.27\text{p} \times 418 = 6382.86\text{p}$
His bill is £63.83

> You are working in pence. Keep writing pence until you change to £.
> Round to the nearest penny.
> He does **not** have a bill of £6382.86!

EXAMPLE

How can you tell these answers are wrong, just by looking at them?
- a $23.5 \times 10 = 23.50$
- b $104.6 \div 100 = 10\,460$

- a The digits have not moved at all.
- b 10 460 is bigger than 104.6 – it should be smaller.

> In **a** a 0 has been added after the decimal point – this makes no difference to the values of the digits.

Exercise AN2

1. Work out
   a $2 \div 1000$
   b $2\,348\,392 \times 10\,000$
   c $0.003\,48 \times 10\,000\,000$

2. There are 12 inches in a foot and 3 feet in a yard.
   There are 1760 yards in 1 mile.
   a How many inches are there in 1 mile?
   b How many yards are there in 2.6 miles?
   c Brett's pace is 0.9 yards long. How many paces does Brett take when he walks for a mile?

3. Explain how you know these answers are wrong just by looking at them.
   a $123 \times 0.4 = 492$
   b $16 \div 0.5 = 8$
   c $48 \times 0.5 = 0.24$
   d $2.3 \times 100 = 2.300$
   e $1.4 \times 10 = 0.14$
   f $0.5 \times 1000 = 600$
   g $8 \div 100 = 0.8$

4. Kobe pays a monthly contract of £25 for his mobile phone. He makes 200 calls in the month. How much is each call costing him on average?

5. Here are some facts about metric lengths.

   > There are 1000 millimetres (mm) in 1 metre (m)
   > 100 centimetres (cm) in 1 metre
   > 1000 metres in 1 kilometre (km).

   a A shelf is 4.2 metres long. How many millimetres is this?
   b Paula walks 1.06 kilometres to school. How many metres is this?
   c A shelf is 140 mm wide. A shelf bracket is 0.1 m wide. Can the bracket be used to hold up the shelf?
   d The head teacher wants to take a picture of all the pupils lined up, shoulder to shoulder, along the school drive. There are 430 pupils in the school. The average width of a pupil across the shoulders is 380 mm. The drive is 150 m long. Can the photograph be taken in a single line?

6. Alan buys a petrol car that emits 0.11 kg of carbon every kilometre. How many kilometres has he driven if the car has emitted 1 tonne of carbon?

   > There are 1000 kg in 1 tonne.

Rounding and approximation

You can **round** a number to the nearest ten or the nearest hundred or thousand.

EXAMPLE

Round these numbers to the nearest ten.
a 2319   b 2313

a 2319 = 2320 to the nearest ten
b 2313 = 2310 to the nearest ten

2313 is nearer to 2310 than 2320 and 2319 is nearer to 2320 than 2310.

When you round to the nearest ten, look at the units digit.
If it is 5 or more, round up. If it is less than 5, round down.

EXAMPLE

Round 2309
a to the nearest hundred   b to the nearest thousand.

a 2309 = 2300 (to nearest 100)
b 2309 = 2000 (to nearest 1000)

Look at the place value of the digit following the one you are rounding. If it is 5 or more, round up. If it is less than 5, round down.

You can round decimal numbers.

EXAMPLE

Round 63.64 to
a the nearest whole number   b one decimal place.

a 63.64 = 64 (to nearest whole number)
b 63.64 = 63.6 (1 dp)

You can round using **significant figures** (sf).
For example   19 783 = 19 800 to 3 sf.

'significant' means important.

Put two zeros to keep the digits in the correct columns.

- The most significant figure is the one with the largest place value.

EXAMPLE

Copy these numbers and underline the most significant figure in each.
a 302 451.6   b 0.000 612   c 2.208   d 0.013 87

a <u>3</u>02 451.6   b 0.000 <u>6</u>12   c <u>2</u>.208   d 0.0<u>1</u>387

The zeros at the start of a decimal number are **not** significant figures.

When you round using significant figures, start at the left-hand side of the number at the first digit that is not zero.

Rounding and approximation

EXAMPLE

Round 0.097 62 to   **a** 3 sf   **b** 2 sf   **c** 1 sf

a 0.09762 = 0.0976 to 3 sf
b 0.09762 = 0.098 to 2 sf
c 0.09762 = 0.1 to 1 sf

> In part **c** the 9 is followed by a 7 so you must round up. When you round up 0.09 you get 0.1

Exercise AN3

1. Write each of these numbers in words.
   a 11 384   b 2 010 345   c 4 500 020   d 23 444 012

2. Write each of these numbers in figures.
   a twelve thousand, six hundred and nine
   b fifty million, one hundred and twenty thousand and seven
   c one hundred and forty-two point two
   d fifteen million, nine hundred and five thousand and fifty-three

3. Copy each number and underline the digit in the decimal place indicated.
   a 12.376 (second dp)   b 0.004 69 (first dp)
   c 25.0936 (third dp)   d 3.5398 (second dp)

4. Round the numbers in question **3** correct to the decimal place indicated.

   > Look at the digit in the next decimal place when you round.

5. Copy each number and underline the first significant figure.
   a 12.376   b 0.004 69   c 25.0936   d 3.5398

6. Round each number as indicated.
   a 140 298   the nearest hundred.   b 34 718   1 sf
   c 0.580 76 1 dp   d 17.099   1 dp
   e 45 970   1 sf   f 1.973 04 2 dp
   g 2.619   1 sf   h 0.002 84 1 sf
   i 825.774   2 dp   j 16.99   1 dp

7. Calculate
   a 13 × 0.13 correct to 1 dp   b 4.56 × 4.56 correct to the nearest whole number
   c 1 ÷ 7 correct to 2 dp   d 12.3 ÷ 1.6 correct to 1 dp

8. Barry bought 16 litres of fuel at 119.9p a litre.
   How much did he pay for this fuel? (Round to the nearest penny.)

9. Chen buys 33 bags of potatoes at 86p a bag. He makes them into chips.
   Each bag of potatoes makes 7 portions of chips.
   a How much does Chen pay for the potatoes?
   b How many portions of chips does he make?
   c What is the cost of the potatoes per portion of chips? (Round to the nearest penny.)
   d How much should he charge for a portion of chips if he wants to make a profit of 8p per portion?
   e How much profit does he make if he sells all the chips he makes?

Rounding and approximation

Factors, multiples and primes

- **A multiple** of a number is any number in that number's multiplication table.
  Multiples of 5 are 5, 10, 15, … (the answers to
  $1 \times 5, 2 \times 5, 3 \times 5, …$)

- A **common multiple** of two (or more) numbers is a multiple of both numbers, for example 28 is a common multiple of 4 and 7.

- The **least common multiple (LCM)** of two (or more) numbers is the lowest number that they both divide into, for example the LCM of 4 and 7 is 28.

EXAMPLE

Find the LCM of 12 and 15.

Multiples of 12: 12, 24, 36, 48, **60**, 72, 84, …
Multiples of 15: 15, 30, 45, **60**, …
The least common multiple of 12 and 15 is 60.

- A **factor** divides exactly into a number.
  1, 2, 3, 4 and 6 are all factors of 12.

- The **highest common factor (HCF)** of two (or more) numbers is the highest number that divides into both of them, for example the HCF of 12 and 18 is 6.

EXAMPLE

Find the highest common factor (HCF) of 42 and 90.

First write each number as the product of prime factors.
$42 = \mathbf{2} \times \mathbf{3} \times 7$ and $90 = \mathbf{2} \times \mathbf{3} \times 3 \times 5$
The HCF of 42 and 90 = $2 \times 3 = 6$

2 and 3 are common factors so the HCF is 2×3

- A **prime number** has only two factors, the number itself and 1.
  Learn this list of the first ten prime numbers.
  2, 3, 5, 7, 11, 13, 17, 19, 23, 29

Notice that 1 is not a prime number (it does not have two factors).

Test to see if a number is prime by dividing it by 2 then 3 then 5 …
If you get a whole number at any point, the number is not prime.

- A **prime factor** is a factor of a number that is also prime. 3 is a factor of 12 and it is prime, so 3 is a prime factor of 12.

2 and 3 are prime factors of 12.

You can write a number as the **product** of its prime factors, for example $24 = 2 \times 2 \times 2 \times 3 = 2^3 \times 3$

EXAMPLE

Write 60 as the product of its prime factors.

$60 = ③ \times 20$
$20 = 4 \times ⑤$
$4 = ② \times ②$
$60 = 2 \times 2 \times 3 \times 5 = 2^2 \times 3 \times 5$

Think of any two whole numbers that multiply to give 60. If one is prime, put a ring round it and repeat the process with the other number until you have only primes.

Exercise AN4

1. Write the first five multiples of each number.
   - **a** 6
   - **b** 8
   - **c** 17
   - **d** 23
   - **e** 51
   - **f** 242

2. Find all the factors of each number.
   - **a** 16
   - **b** 21
   - **c** 36
   - **d** 43
   - **e** 120
   - **f** 552

3. Find all the prime numbers between 30 and 50.

4. Work out whether each number is prime or not. Show your working.
   - **a** 27
   - **b** 83
   - **c** 123
   - **d** 117
   - **e** 215
   - **f** 401

5. Write each number as the product of its prime factors.
   - **a** 30
   - **b** 72
   - **c** 98
   - **d** 130
   - **e** 166
   - **f** 1024

6. For each of the following, find the least common multiple.
   - **a** 12 and 30
   - **b** 16 and 24
   - **c** 22 and 12
   - **d** 6, 15 and 20
   - **e** 9, 12 and 15

7. Find the highest common factor of each set of numbers in question **6**.

8. Two model cars start together at 9 o'clock on a track.
   One takes 10 seconds to complete the track and the other takes 12 seconds.
   At what time will they next pass each other on the starting line?

Factors, multiples and primes

Calculator skills

You will need to practise with your own calculator as not all calculators have the same functions on their keys.

- The **square** key is usually x^2

  The **cube** key is usually x^3

  Enter a number, press the key and then $=$

- The **square root** key is usually $\sqrt{\blacksquare}$

  If you have to **square root a whole calculation** then you may have to put brackets round the calculation first.
  To find $\sqrt{64-21}$ you enter
  $\sqrt{(64-21)} =$ and the answer is 6.5574...

  If you leave out the brackets you may get −13, which is wrong. You may have to round the answer.

- The **cube root** key is usually $\sqrt[3]{\blacksquare}$

  Use this like the square root key.

- The **reciprocal** of a number is 1 ÷ the number.

  The key is usually x^{-1}

If you have **a calculation written as a fraction**, put brackets round the top and bottom of the fraction and remember that a fraction is a division.

To find $\dfrac{23.4 - 6.27}{1.2 \times 2}$

If you leave out the brackets, you may get 12.95, which is wrong.

write $\dfrac{(23.4 - 6.27)}{(1.2 \times 2)}$ and enter $(23.4 - 6.27) \div (1.2 \times 2) =$

The answer is 7.1375

EXAMPLE

Calculate the cost of one ticket if 15 tickets cost £18.

18 ÷ 15 = 1.2 = £1.20

EXAMINER'S TIP

Never write 1.2 for money, always £1.20

EXAMPLE

Bryony makes a solid cube by joining lots of 1 cm cubes together.
The cube is 6 cm along each edge. How many cubes has she used?

$6^3 = 216$ cubes

EXAMINER'S TIP

6^3 is tidier than $6 \times 6 \times 6$

Exercise AN5

MEDIUM

1. Use your calculator to work out the following.
   Round to 1 dp if the answer is not exact.

   a 2.5^2
   b $\sqrt{625}$
   c $1.4^3 - 1.4^2$

   d $\sqrt[3]{1331}$
   e $\dfrac{(2.6+1.9)}{1.5}$
   f $\dfrac{4.6^2 - 2}{(5.1+2.3-3.4)}$

   g $\sqrt[3]{6.1^2 - 0.81}$
   h $\dfrac{\sqrt{2.5 \times 4}}{5^2}$
   i $\dfrac{4.5^3 + 1.3^2}{1.4 - 2}$

2. Calculate the **reciprocal** of these numbers.

   a 5
   b 0.2
   c 12
   d 100
   e 18
   f 0.08

   What do you notice about the answers to **a** and **b**?

3. Darren buys 6 rolls of loft insulation.
   Each roll is a 5 m length of insulation and is 400 mm wide.
   He pays £77.94 for all six rolls.
   a What is the cost of 1 m of loft insulation?
   b What is the cost of insulation for 4 m² of the loft?

4. This formula can be used to change between miles and kilometres.

   distance in miles ⟶ ×1.6 ⟶ distance in kilometres

   Change
   a 14 miles into kilometres
   b 32 kilometres into miles.

5. A bag contains 1.8 kilograms of sugar.
   Gemma uses 560 grams of the sugar to make
   a cake and 196 g to fill her sugar bowl.
   How much sugar is left in the bag?

   > There are 1000 grams in 1 kilogram.

6. Imani earns 2 loyalty points every time she spends £1 at Supersave. She can exchange 100 loyalty points for £0.50. Imani cashes in all her loyalty points at Christmas and receives £46. How much money has she spent to earn these points?

Calculator skills

Order of operations

BIDMAS tells you the order in which to do a calculation. All scientific calculators use these rules **but** you still need to check your answers in case of error.

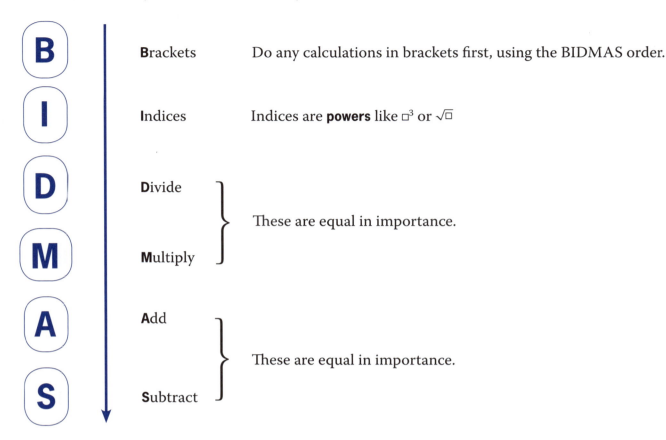

B	**B**rackets	Do any calculations in brackets first, using the BIDMAS order.
I	**I**ndices	Indices are **powers** like $\square^3$ or $\sqrt{\square}$
D	**D**ivide	These are equal in importance.
M	**M**ultiply	
A	**A**dd	These are equal in importance.
S	**S**ubtract	

If all the signs are equal in value, then work from left to right.

- When a calculation is a fraction, it is the same as division, so $\dfrac{5}{8}$ is the same as $5 \div 8$.

For a calculation like $\dfrac{12+6}{5-3}$ you must put brackets in when you use a calculator. This becomes $(12 + 6) \div (5 - 3) = 9$
Try it on your calculator without brackets and you will get 10.2 ✗

You may be given a calculation in your exam and asked to put brackets in to make the answer correct.
Write the calculation in the working space and try brackets in different places to get the answer. Only write the brackets in the **answer space** when you have got it right.

EXAMPLE

Put brackets in this calculation to make it correct.
$6 \times 5 - 1 + 3 = 27$

The answer to the calculation without using brackets is 32.
Try $6 \times 5 - (1 + 3)$ ✗   The answer is 26 …… **try it yourself**

EXAMPLE

1 Calculate   a $3.4 + 1.2 \times 5$ b $(5 - 1.2)^2$ c $\dfrac{14.3 - 4^2}{5 + 3}$

2 Put brackets in this calculation to make the answer correct.
$15 - 2 \times 7 + 3 = -5$

EXAMINER'S TIP

$5 - 1.2$ is in a bracket so is done first.

---

1 a $3.4 + 1.2 \times 5 = 3.4 + 6 = 9.4$ b $(5 - 1.2)^2 = 3.8^2 = 14.44$

   c $\dfrac{(14.3 - 4^2)}{(5+3)} = \dfrac{-1.7}{8} = -0.2125$ or -0.21 to 2dp

2 Try $(15 - 2) \times 7 + 3$ The answer is 94
   Try $15 - 2 \times (7 + 3)$ The answer is -5 so this is correct

EXAMINER'S TIP

When you enter this in your calculator, type

$(14.3 - 4 \boxed{X^2}) \div (5 + 3)$

EXAMINER'S TIP

There is no point trying $15 - (2 \times 7) + 3$ because this is the same order of operations as in the question.

Exercise AN6

MEDIUM

1 Use your calculator to work out the following.
   a $2.1 + 5.8 \times 3$
   b $4.2 - 2.6 \div 2$
   c $(1 + 4.3) \times 3 - 6.1$
   d $4 - 2 \times (3.4 + 1.2)$
   e $3 - (2 \times 1.4 + 1)$
   f $12 + 2(3.3 \times 4) - 2$

2 Do a rough calculation to check the answers to question **1**. Part **a** is done for you.
   a
   $2 + 6 \times 3$
   $= 2 + 18$
   $= 20$

3 Use your calculator to work out the following. Give the answer to 1dp where necessary.
   a $\dfrac{3 \times 5}{1 + 2}$
   b $\dfrac{(1.3 + 2 \times 3.7)}{1.3 + 0.2}$
   c $\dfrac{3 \times 5.2 - 4.5}{3.2 - 2}$
   d $\dfrac{(10.2 - 3.1 \times 2.4)}{2.2 + 1.6}$
   e $\dfrac{3^2 \times 5}{1 + 2^2}$
   f $\sqrt{(12.3 + 4.7)}$
   g $\dfrac{\sqrt{18.8 - 9.8} + 9.6}{1 + 2}$
   h $\dfrac{(6+8)^2}{2.5^2 - 1.5^2}$

4 Put brackets in the appropriate place in each calculation to give the answer.
   a $1 + 2 \times 3 = 9$
   b $1 + 2 \times 3 - 4 = -1$
   c $10 - 3 + 2 \times 5 = -15$
   d $10 - 3 + 2 \times 5 = 45$
   e $10 - 3 + 2 \times 5 = -3$
   f $14 + 5 \times 2^2 = 76$
   g $14 + 5 \times 2^2 = 114$
   h $12 - 2 + 5 \times 2 + 1 = 1$

5 a What is the answer to Sally's calculation?
   b Write the calculation in the form of a fraction and remember to include brackets.

   Sally says:
   Add 12 and 3, double the answer and then divide the result by 10. What is the answer?

6 Sarah the electrician charges a 'call out' fee of £25 and then £15 for each half hour she works.
   Owen calls Sarah to mend his immersion heater. The job takes 90 minutes.
   Owen works out what he thinks he will pay like this: $(£25 + £15) \times 3 = £120$
   a Is Owen right?
   b What calculation should Owen have done?
   c What was Owen's real bill?

Order of operations

Basic ratio

A ratio **compares the sizes** of two or more amounts.
A family has six pet animals.
Four animals are dogs (D) and two animals are cats (C) so D : C = 4 : 2.
There are twice as many dogs as cats, so the ratio can also be written D : C = 2 : 1.

- Amounts must be in the same units to write a ratio.

    If A = 1 kg and B = 500 g A : B is not 1 : 500.
    Change A to 1000 g and A : B = 1000 : 500.
    (This means that A is twice as big as B.)

- A ratio does not have any units because it compares relative amounts.

    EXAMINER'S TIP
    A : B = 3 kg : 2 kg ✗
    But A : B = 3 : 2 ✓

A : B = 3 : 2 means that for every three shares of B there are two shares of A.
So, A is $1\frac{1}{2}$ times as big as B ($3 = 2 \times 1\frac{1}{2}$).

Here are five ways you can change a ratio.

1. **Simplify** the ratio by dividing each share by a common factor.

    12 : 4 = 3 : 1 (÷4)

2. Multiply each share by the same number. This does not change the meaning of the ratio.
    2 : 1 = 6 : 3 (× 3) The first number is still twice as big as the second one.

    2 : 1 = 6 : 3 (×3)

3. Write the ratio in the form **1 : n**.
    Divide all the shares by the share that is to become 1.

    6 : 27 = 1 : 4.5 (÷6)

4. Change the ratio to a fraction by writing one share as a fraction of the whole amount (all the shares).
    a. Add up all the shares. This is the denominator.
    b. Write the one share as the numerator.

    3 : 4   3 + 4 = 7
    $\frac{3}{7}$ $\left(\text{or } \frac{4}{7}\right)$

5. Change the ratio to a fraction by writing one share as a fraction of another share.
    a. The one share is the numerator.
    b. Write the second share as the denominator.

    3 : 4
    $\frac{3}{4}$ $\left(\text{or } \frac{4}{3}\right)$

EXAMPLE

a. Simplify F : G : H = 4 : 6 : 10
b. Simplify H : J = 1.4 : 0.9

Divide by 2.
This is like cancelling fractions.
Always check that there are no more common factors to divide by.

a. F : G : H = 2 : 3 : 5   b. H : J = 14 : 9

Multiply by 10 so there are no decimals.

EXAMPLE

Write P : Q = 4 : 5 in the form 1 to n.

P : Q = 1 : 1.25

P has to be 1, so divide both shares by 4.

14   Basic ratio

EXAMPLE

Sue, Terry and Unity are left some money.
They divide it between them in the ratio S : T : U = 2 : 3 : 5
 a What fraction does Sue have of the whole amount?
 b What fraction is Sue's share of Unity's share?

 a There are 2 + 3 + 5 = 10 shares
   Sue has $\frac{2}{10}$ or $\frac{1}{5}$ of all the shares.
 b Sue has 2 shares and Unity has 5.
   Sue has $\frac{2}{5}$ of Unity's share.

EXAMINER'S TIP

Always check that you have cancelled the fractions as far as possible and there are no other common factors.

2 and 5 have no common factors so cannot be cancelled.

Exercise AN7

MEDIUM

Questions like this may appear in your examination paper. However, you will not be asked lots of similar questions on the same topic.
A single part of one of questions **1** to **6** could form a single examination question.

1 Write each ratio as simply as possible using only whole numbers.
 a P : Q = 10 : 15
 b G : M = 12 : 9
 c R : P = 24 : 36
 d K : J = 3.6 : 1.2
 e A : B : C = 20 : 30 : 40
 f A : G : P = 45 : 18 : 54
 g R : U : F = 2.4 : 0.6 : 1.8
 h J : K = 1.5 : 2
 i S : H : G = 12 : 1.5 : 4
 j P : S = 5 : 0.5

2 Write each ratio in the form 1 : n.
 a S : T = 3 : 12
 b G : H = 10 : 5
 c F : K = 1.2 : 1.8
 d J : G = 240 : 600
 e L : K = 9 : 1.8
 f P : M = 20 : 4.4

3 Write each ratio in the form n : 1.
 a K : P = 25 : 20
 b H : S = 1 : 2.5
 c G : Y = 24 : 19.2
 d B : G = 14.2 : 8.52
 e S : Y = 3 : 0.5
 f M : T = 4.2 : 4.8

4 In each case write the ratio A : B, giving your answer in its simplest form.
 a A = 5 kg   B = 12 kg
 b A = 5 kg   B = 1500 g
 c A = 12 minutes   B = 1 hour
 d A = £10   B = 50p
 e A = 3 days   B = 3 weeks
 f A = 25 cm   B = 1.2 m

5 In each case write the ratio A : B : C, giving your answer in its simplest form.
 a A = £2   B = 75p   C = £1.50
 b A = 4 litres   B = 6 litres   C = 500 millilitres
 c A = 10 cm   B = 0.2 m   C = 1 m
 d A = 40 mm   B = 2 cm   C = 1 m
 e A = £24   B = 5p   C = £5.50
 f A = 5 hours   B = 20 minutes   C = $1\frac{1}{2}$ hours

6 a S : R = 2 : 5. What fraction is S of R?
 b G : K : P = 1 : 3 : 4. What fraction is P of the total?
 c M : V = 9 : 5. What fraction is V of M?
 d A : H : Y = 3 : 2 : 6. What fraction is A of Y?
 e G : H : T = 1 : 2 : 5. What fraction is H of T?
 f P : G : X = 4 : 6 : 5. What fraction is P of the total?

Basic ratio

Using ratio

AN8

You can use ratios to find the solutions to problems.

To share an amount in a ratio
- Add up all the shares of the ratio.
- Divide the amount by the total number of shares
- Multiply each share by the given ratio.

Share £2000 in the ratio 2 : 3
$2 + 3 = 5$
$2000 ÷ 5 = 400$
$400 × 2 = £800$
$400 × 3 = £1200$

EXAMPLE

Divide 2.4 kg in the ratio M : N = 3 : 5.

$3 + 5 = 8$ (Add all the shares)
$2.4 \text{ kg} ÷ 8 = 0.3 \text{ kg}$ (Find the value of 1 share)
$M = 3 × 0.3 \text{ kg} = 0.9 \text{ kg}$ and
$N = 5 × 0.3 \text{ kg} = 1.5 \text{ kg}$

EXAMINER'S TIP

Check that all the weights add up to the whole amount (2.4 kg).
(0.9 + 1.5 = 2.4 ✓)

To find the original amount when you know one share
- Add up all the shares
- Divide the known value by the size of **its** share
- Multiply these two amount together.

You can also find the size of each of the other shares. After the second step, just multiply the weight of one share by the number of each other share.

EXAMINER'S TIP

This could be where ingredients are mixed in a ratio. You will know the weight of one of the ingredients and the ratio. You have to find the weight of the others.

EXAMPLE

Peter uses his phone to make texts and calls.
The ratio of the number of calls to the number of texts is 7 : 5.
He sends 140 texts. How many calls does he make?

1 share = $140 ÷ 5 = 28$ (Find the value of 1 share)
Number of calls = $28 × 7 = 196$ (Calls has **7** shares)

EXAMPLE

A recipe uses flour, sugar and butter in the ratio 5 : 3 : 2 by weight. 75 g of sugar is used.
- **a** What weight of each ingredient is used?
- **b** What is the total weight of the mixture?

a   1 share = $75 \text{ g} ÷ 3 = 25 \text{ g}$ (Find the value of 1 share)
     Amount of flour $5 × 25 \text{ g} = 125 \text{ g}$ (Flour has **5** shares)
     Amount of butter $2 × 25 \text{ g} = 50 \text{ g}$ (Butter has **2** shares)
b   Total weight = $25\text{g} × (5 + 3 + 2) = 25 \text{ g} × 10 = 250 \text{ g}$

EXAMINER'S TIP

Check that total weight = sum of shares.
250 g = 75 g + 125 g + 50 g ✓

Exercise AN8

1. In each case, divide the amount in the ratio given.
   a £25 in the ratio A : B = 1 : 4
   b 200 g in the ratio A : B = 7 : 3
   c 2.8 kg in the ratio A : B = 3 : 5
   d 3 hours in the ratio A : B : C = 5 : 3 : 1

2. a Find the total amount when A = 4.5 kg and A : B = 5 : 4.
   b Find G when A = £6.40 and A : G = 5 : 8.
   c Find P when S = 30p and P : S = 12 : 5.
   d Find W and X when Z = 4 litres and W : X : Z = 1 : 15 : 8.

3. John and Andrew take part in a sponsored walk.
   a The amounts they raise are in the ratio John : Andrew = 4 : 5.
     John raises £48.60.
     i How much does Andrew raise?   ii How much do they raise altogether?
   b The amount they raise is $\frac{3}{40}$ of the total amount raised.
     How much is raised altogether?

4. Paula's garden is divided into lawn (L), flowers (F), paths (P) and vegetables (V) in the ratio L : F : P : V = 10 : 6 : 3 : 8.
   The area of the lawn is 45 m².
   a What area is planted with vegetables?
   b What fraction of the garden is flowers?

5. A wholemeal biscuit weighs 12.5 g and contains the following nutrients.
   a What is the weight of the 'Other' nutrients?
   b What is the ratio of carbohydrate to fat?
   c What is the ratio of fat : fibre?
   d Explain what your answer to part c tells you about the amounts of fat : fibre in these biscuits.
   e The maker of the biscuits claims, 'Less than $\frac{1}{10}$ of our biscuit is fat'. Explain whether this is true.

Carbohydrate	7.0 g
Fat	1.2 g
Fibre	1.8 g
Other	2.5 g

6. Connor uses his car for work (W) and pleasure (P).
   The ratio of the miles he drives is W : P = 4 : 3.
   One month he drives 1470 miles.
   a How many miles does he drive for pleasure?

   Connor spends £160.80 buying fuel for all his driving that month.
   He claims 40p a mile from his company for the miles that he drives for work.
   b Does the money he claims cover the cost of the petrol he buys?

7. Shades of pink paint can be made by mixing red (R) and white (W) paint in these ratios by volume.
   The more white is used, the paler the colour.

Name	Sunset	Rose	Pale	Hint
Ratio R : W	5 : 3	5 : 2	6 : 1	25 : 3

   a Which ratio makes the darkest pink?
   b If Gretta wants 3 litres of 'Sunset', what volume of red and what volume of white paint will she need to mix?
   c Alan mixes 1.2 litres of red with 200 ml of white. Which shade has he made?
   d Karen wants to mix 'Hint' and has 600 ml of white.
     If she uses all of this, with the correct amount of red to make the paint, what volume of 'Hint' has she made?

Using ratio

Symbols

AA1

- In an **equation** a letter represents a specific unknown number.
  You **solve** an equation by finding the value of the letter.
  For example in the equation $5x = 20$ the value of $x = 4$

  An equation always has an = sign.

- An **expression** is a collection of terms separated by + or − signs.
  $3x + y - x$ is an expression

  An expression never has an = sign.

- A **formula** tells you how two (or more) different quantities are related.
  For example, the formula $A = \pi d$ tells you that the area of a circle is related to its diameter.
  You can substitute the value of either A or d into the formula to find the corresponding value of d or A.

  A formula contains two or more letters.

- Expressions can be simplified by collecting **like terms** or using powers.

EXAMPLE

Simplify
- **a** $r \times r \times r \times r \times r$
- **b** $5k + 2k$
- **c** $6p + 5r + 3p - 4r$

- **a** $r \times r \times r \times r \times r = r^5$
- **b** $5k + 2k = 7k$
- **c** $6p + 5r + 3p - 4r = 9p + r$

Write r rather than 1r.

EXAMPLE

Decide whether the following are equations, expressions or formulae.
- **a** $3m + 2n$
- **b** $3m + 6 = 18$
- **c** $v = u + at$
- **d** $\dfrac{r}{2} = r + 2$

- **a** $3m + 2n$ is an expression – it has no = sign.
- **b** $3m + 6 = 18$ is an equation.
- **c** $v = u + at$ is a formula.
- **d** $\dfrac{r}{2} = r + 2$ is an equation.

Exercise AA1

LOW

1. Write each statement as a single amount. Use a letter to represent each item. For example, 6 apples + 2 apples can be written as 6a + 2a = 8a.
   - a 8 apples + 7 apples
   - b 6 boys + 5 boys
   - c 3 CDs + 5 CDs
   - d 8 chairs and 13 chairs
   - e 9 toys and 23 toys
   - f 18 books + 8 books
   - g 13 chocolates − 8 chocolates
   - h 6 cakes − 6 cakes
   - i 15 sweets − 7 sweets
   - j 13 bananas − 6 bananas

2. Simplify these expressions.
   - a $m + m + m$
   - b $n + n + n + n + n + n + n$
   - c $y + y + y + y + y + y$
   - d $z + z + z − z + z$

3. Collect the terms and simplify each expression.
   - a $6a + 7a$
   - b $5n + 12n$
   - c $6t + 9t$
   - d $3x + 16x$
   - e $9r − 5r$
   - f $6f − 2f$
   - g $12g − 5g$
   - h $15r − 7r$
   - i $16n + 4n + 3n$
   - j $6c + 8c + 3c$

4. Write each of these as a single term.
   - a $4 \times m$
   - b $p \times 3$
   - c $r \times s$
   - d $12 \times q$
   - e $5 \times g$
   - f $c \times 4$
   - g $d \times 8$
   - h $j \times k$
   - i $n \times n$
   - j $e \times 15$
   - k $t \times t$
   - l $6 \times m \times n$

5. Simplify each expression.
   - a $8n + 3n + 4n$
   - b $3m + 2m + 7m$
   - c $8p + 6p + 3p$
   - d $5q + 7q + 6q$
   - e $12x − 7x − 4x$
   - f $8w − w − 3w$
   - g $4a + 6a − 3a$
   - h $12b − 3b − 4b$
   - i $3j − 4j + 2j$
   - j $k − 5k + 6k$

6. Simplify these divisions. The first one is done for you.
   - a $d \div 4 = \dfrac{d}{4}$
   - b $x \div 3$
   - c $y \div 7$
   - d $t \div 9$
   - e $2a \div 3$
   - f $3n \div 4$
   - g $5p \div 7$
   - h $2v \div 4$

7. Use these four terms and three signs to make the different totals.

   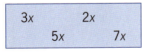   

   - a $13x$
   - b $3x$
   - c $7x$
   - d $11x$

8. Simplify
   - a $b + b + b$
   - b $3v + 2v + 6v$
   - c $y + 6y + 2y − 5y$
   - d $c \times c \times c \times c$
   - e $2s + 5t + 7s + 8t$
   - f $7j + 2k − 3j + 5k$
   - g $4 \times z \times z \times z$
   - h $4g − 2h − 5g − 7h$
   - i $6q + r − 5q − 5r + 4r − q$

9. Decide whether the following are equations, expressions or formulae.
   - a $8 − 2f = 10$
   - b $2r + 10$
   - c $A = 4\pi r^2$
   - d $v^2 = u^2 + 2as$
   - e $y = 8y + 21$
   - f $8x + 9y − 6z$

Coordinates

AA2

- The point (0, 0) on a graph where the axes cross is called the **origin**.
- The **coordinates** of a point P, for example (5, 2), tell you that P is 5 units along and 2 units up from the origin (0, 0).
- The first number, 5, is the **x-coordinate**.
- The second number, 2, is the **y-coordinate**.

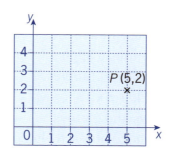

EXAMPLE

a Mark and label these points on a grid.
   $A(2, 3)$, $B(-3, 1)$ and $C(-3, -3)$
b Write down the coordinates of point D such that $ABCD$ is a parallelogram.

a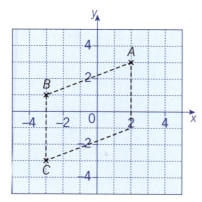

b D is at $(2, -1)$

EXAMINER'S TIP

When marking points, use a small neat cross and write labels nearby. If you just write the letter on the point it may not be accurate enough.

EXAMINER'S TIP

It is OK to join up the points even if the question does not ask you to.

- The **midpoint** of a line is halfway between the ends.
- The length of a line can be calculated using Pythagoras' theorem.

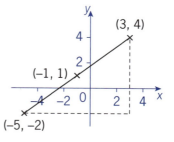

EXAMPLE

Point A is at $(-2, 1)$, point B is at $(6, 4)$.
a Calculate the length of line AB, giving your answer to 3 significant figures.
b Find the midpoint of AB.

Start by drawing a sketch.
a By Pythagoras: $c^2 = a^2 + b^2$
   $c^2 = 8^2 + 3^2 = 64 + 9 = 73$
   $c = \sqrt{73} = 8.54$ units

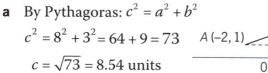

Technically AB should be called a line segment, as a line is infinitely long.

$\sqrt{73}$ is an 'exact' answer.
8.54 is correct to 3 significant figures.

b The midpoint is at $\left(\dfrac{-2+6}{2}, \dfrac{1+4}{2}\right) = (2, 2.5)$

You can think of the midpoint as the 'mean average' point.

Exercise AA2

MEDIUM

1 Write down the coordinates of points *A* to *H*.

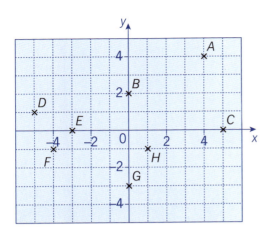

2 **a** Mark and label these points on a grid.
       P(3, 5), *Q*(−2, 4) and *R*(−2, 0)
   b *PQRS* is a trapezium.
       Find two possible positions for point S. Each coordinate must be a whole number.

3 Pete marks the points *U*(−3, 1) and *V*(5, 1) on a grid.
   He finds the point *W* so that *UVW* is an isosceles triangle.
   He says that *W* must always have 1 as its *x*-coordinate.
   Jennie disagrees.
   Find a possible point for *W* so that Jennie can demonstrate to Pete that he is wrong.

4 For each of these pairs of points, *A* and *B*,
   i find the midpoint of *AB*
   ii find the length of *AB*. Give your answer to 3 significant figures where appropriate.
   a *A*(1, 1) *B*(4, 5)   **b** *A*(1, 4) *B*(7, 0)
   c *A*(−1, −4) *B*(6, 2)   **d** *A*(2, −3) *B*(−4, −1)
   e *A*(−5, −2) *B*(3, 13) **f** *A*(0, −2) *B*(7, 0)

5 *PQRS* is a rectangle.
   P, *Q* and *R* are the points (−1, −2), (1, 4) and (7, 2) respectively.
   a Find the coordinates of point *S*.

   M is the midpoint of *PQ* and *N* is the midpoint of *QR*.
   b Show that the length of *MN* is exactly $\sqrt{20}$.

Coordinates

Formulae

AA3

- A **formula** tells you how two (or more) quantities are related.

A formula can be in words or letters.

For example, the formula $A = \pi r^2$ tells you that the area of a circle, A, is π times the square of its radius, r.

- You can **substitute** values into a formula.

For example, if $y = 3x - 10$ find y when $x = 6$.
$y = 3 \times 6 - 10 = 18 - 10 = 8$

- You can **derive** (write in letters) a formula using information you know.

*The letter on its own is called the **subject** of the formula.*
P is the subject of the formula
P = 4l

For example, the perimeter of a square of side l is given by the formula
$P = 4l$

l

- You can **rearrange** or **change the subject** of a formula by doing the same operation to both sides.

For example, make p the subject of the formula
$r = 3p + q$
$r - q = 3p$ Subtract q from both sides
$p = \dfrac{r-q}{3}$ Divide both sides by 3

EXAMPLE

Hanif hires a carpet cleaner from *Coventry Cleaners*.
The hire charge, in £, is worked out using this word formula:
    Charge = 20 + (number of days hire × 8) + (number of litres of cleaning fluid used × 5)

a   Hanif hires the carpet cleaner for 3 days and uses 12 litres of cleaning fluid. How much is the charge?

b   Write a formula for the total charge C, if he hires it for d days and uses c litres of cleaning fluid.

a   Charge = 20 + 3 × 8 + 12 × 5   b $C = 20 + 8d + 5c$
           = 20 + 24 + 60 = £104

EXAMPLE

If $s = 3t + 2u$, find s when $t = 4$ and $u = -2$.

$s = 3t + 2u$
$= 3 \times 4 + 2 \times -2$
$= 12 - 4$
$= 8$

Remember the correct order of operations: × before +.
Also remember the rules
+ × + = +
− × − = + and
+ × − = −

Formulae

EXAMPLE

Rearrange these formulae to make p the subject.

a $s = \dfrac{p}{r}$ **b** $t = \dfrac{p-s}{r}$

a $s = \dfrac{p}{r}$

$rs = p$ Multiply both sides by r

b $t = \dfrac{p-s}{r}$

$tr = p - s$ Multiply both sides by r

$tr + s = p$ Add s to both sides

> Compare the operations used here to those in solving equations. The processes are very similar.

Exercise AA3 — MEDIUM

1 A water company charges its customers for water using the following formula.

cost = standing charge + (cost per cubic metre × number of cubic metres used)

Karl uses 157 cubic metres of water in one year.
The standing charge is £27 and the cost per cubic metre is £1.41.
How much does he pay for his water?

2 If $p = 6$ and $q = 3$, find the value of w if

   a $w = 2p + q$ **b** $w = 8p + 3q$ **c** $w = pq$

   d $w = 2p - q$ **e** $w = 2p - 7q$ **f** $w = \dfrac{p+q}{9}$

3 a A window cleaner charges £p for each window she cleans plus an extra £4. Write a formula for the amount she charges, £C, for cleaning w windows.

   b Write down a formula for the shaded area of this window.

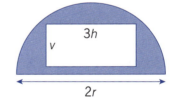

4 Rearrange these formulae to make x the subject.

   a $y = ax$ **b** $m = x - t$ **c** $p = \dfrac{x}{r}$ **d** $k = x + z$

   e $a = 5x - 7$ **f** $y = mx + c$ **g** $t = wx - g$ **h** $s = ab + rx$

   i $q = r(x - z)$ **j** $f = 3m - x$ **k** $p = \dfrac{y}{x}$ **l** $c = \dfrac{x}{t} - d$

5 a The area of an ellipse is given by the formula $A = \pi ab$ where a and b are the lengths shown in the diagram. Rearrange the formula $A = \pi ab$ to make a the subject.

   b A machine cuts ellipses out of a rectangular sheet of metal, 40 cm by 50 cm, to make cases for thermometers.
The ellipses have $a = 3$ cm and $b = 5$ cm.
The axes of symmetry of the ellipses have to be parallel to the edges of the sheet of metal.

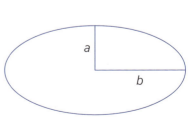

Calculate how much more area of metal is wasted if the ellipses are cut with b parallel to the 50 cm side rather than the 40 cm side.
Explain why this calculation may not be accurate in real life.

Formulae

Sequences

AA4

You should be able to continue sequences and explain the pattern.

> **EXAMPLE**
>
> Find the next two terms in these sequences and explain how you worked them out.
> **a** 5   9   13   17   ...   ...
> **b** 160   80   40   20   ...   ...
>
> ---
>
> **a** 21   25   Add 4 each time.
> **b** 10   5   Divide by 2 each time.

- Sequences are described by a **term-to-term rule** or a **position-to-term rule**.

You can generate a sequence with an nth term by putting $n = 1, 2, 3, \ldots$ and so on in the position-to-term rule.
The first three terms of the sequence with nth term $n^2 + 3$ are
$1^2 + 3 = \mathbf{4}, \quad 2^2 + 3 = \mathbf{7}, \quad 3^2 + 3 = \mathbf{12}$.

- A **linear sequence** is one where the term-to-term rule is to add the same number on each time.
  7, 11, 15, 19, ... ← Here 4 is added each time.

You can find the **nth term** (position-to-term rule) of a linear sequence by looking at the differences.
The nth term of 7, 11, 15, 19, ... is $4n + 3$.

You should be familiar with these sequences:

Odd and even numbers	Squares 1, 4, 9, 16, ...	Cubes 1, 8, 27, 64, ...
Triangle numbers 1, 3, 6, 10, 15, ...	Fibonacci numbers 1, 1, 2, 3, 5, 8, 13, ...	Primes 2, 3, 5, 7, 11, ← 1 is not a prime number.

> **EXAMPLE**
>
> Calculate the 1st term and the 10th term of the sequence with nth term $3n - 2$.
>
> ---
>
> 1st term = $3 \times 1 - 2$ 10th term = $3 \times 10 - 2$
>   = 1   = 30 − 2
>   = 28

EXAMPLE

Find the nth term of the sequence with first five terms
    11, 17, 23, 29, 35, ...

Look at the differences between the terms.

11 17 23
  +6 +6

The sequence goes up in 6s so the nth term starts $6n$.
Look at the first few terms of the sequence with nth term $6n$, that is 6, 12, 18, ...
The terms we want are all 5 more than these.
So the nth term is $6n + 5$.

EXAMINER'S TIP

Don't be like the many candidates who just write '+6' on the answer line and score nothing.

Exercise AA4   — MEDIUM

1 Write the next two terms of each of these sequences.
Explain how you worked out your answer.
   a 11 14 17 20
   b 3 6 12 24
   c 33 27 21 15
   d 243 81 27 9
   e 38 30 22 14
   f 72 36 18 9

2 Write the first two terms of the sequences with these nth terms.
   a $5n + 11$
   b $7n + 1$
   c $10n$
   d $0.2n + 1.4$
   e $12 - 2n$
   f $40 - 2n$
   g $n^2 + n$
   h $n^3 - 2^n$

3 Find the 8th term of the sequences with these nth terms.
   a $12n - 9$
   b $8 - n$

4 a Draw the next L shape in this pattern.
   b Copy and complete this table to show the number of shaded squares.

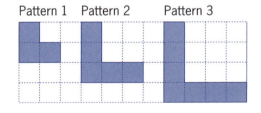

Pattern 1   Pattern 2   Pattern 3

Pattern	1	2	3	4
Number of squares	3	5		

   c How many squares will be shaded in Pattern 100?

5

1 Hexagon   2 Hexagons   3 Hexagons

Find a formula for the number of lines in a similar pattern of n hexagons.

6 Marcus is adding 10 g weights onto a spring. He measures the length of the spring after he has added each weight. Here are his results.

Number of 10 g weights added	1	2	3	4
Length of spring (cm)	38	41.5	45	48.5

   a Explain how Marcus can tell that there is a linear relationship between the number of weights and the length of the spring.
   b Find a formula for the length of the spring when n weights have been added.
   c How many weights must Marcus add to make the spring 1 metre long?

Equations

AA5

You can **solve** an **equation** to find the value of an unknown quantity.

$3x + 1 = 10$ Find the value of x

You should apply the same operation to each side of the equation so that it still balances.

$3x + 1 - 1 = 10 - 1$ Subtract 1 from each side

Full working:
$3x + 1 = 10$
$3x = 9$ Subtract 1 from each side
$x = 3$ Divide both sides by 3
The **solution** is $x = 3$

EXAMPLE

Solve these equations.

a $5x = 40$ **b** $x + 12 = 5$ **c** $4x - 7 = 3$

EXAMINER'S TIP

Equations in the exam will often have solutions that are negative or fractions.

a $5x = 40$
$x = \dfrac{40}{5}$ Divide both sides by 5
$x = 8$

b $x + 12 = 5$
$x = 5 - 12$ Subtract 12 from each side
$x = -7$

c $4x - 7 = 3$
$4x = 10$ Add 7 to both sides
$x = \dfrac{10}{4}$ Divide both sides by 4
$x = 2\dfrac{1}{2}$

You can check your answer by substituting your solution into each side of the equation and seeing if you get the same number. Try it with this example and you should get 3 on each side.

EXAMPLE

Solve these equations.

a $5x + 6 = 2x - 9$ **b** $\dfrac{6m + 7}{2} = 5$

a $5x + 6 = 2x - 9$
$3x + 6 = -9$ Subtract $2x$ from each side
$3x = -15$ Subtract 6 from each side
$x = -5$ Divide each side by 3

b $\dfrac{6m + 7}{2} = 5$
$6m + 7 = 10$ Multiply each side by 2
$6m = 3$ Subtract 7 from each side
$m = \dfrac{1}{2}$ Divide each side by 6

EXAMPLE

Form and solve an equation to find g.

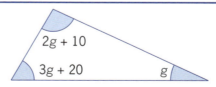

Because angles in a triangle add to 180°,
$g + 2g + 10 + 3g + 20 = 180$
$6g + 30 = 180$
$6g = 150$
$g = 25°$

EXAMINER'S TIP

When questions say 'Form and solve', the answer by itself will not score full marks.

Exercise AA5

MEDIUM

1 Solve these equations.

a $8x = 32$
b $x - 12 = 7$
c $\dfrac{x}{5} = 12$

d $x + 15 = 22$
e $7 = 2x$
f $x + 9 = 5$

g $2w - 3 = 11$
h $\dfrac{x}{4} - 11 = 9$
i $3n + 6 = 3$

j $7x + 5 = 40$
k $11 = 4k - 3$
l $12 - x = 8$

m $\dfrac{x}{5} = 15$
n $\dfrac{24}{x} = 3$
o $20 - 2d = 30$

p $5x + 2 = 2x + 17$
q $8x - 9 = 2x + 15$
r $5x + 4 = 3x + 11$

s $20 - 3x = 2x + 5$
t $9x + 15 = 5x - 1$
u $8x + 9 = 5x$

v $\dfrac{7y + 6}{4} = 12$
w $1 = \dfrac{3m + 8}{2}$
x $\dfrac{6 - x}{5} = 5$

2 a Jo hires a carpet cleaner from this company for 3 hours. How much does it cost her?

b Alex is charged £38 to hire a carpet cleaner for h hours. Form and solve an equation in h to find how long he hired the carpet cleaner for.

> Karl's Carpet Cleaner hire
> £2 per hour
> +
> £10

3 The angles of a quadrilateral are $5x$, $10x$, $4x + 12$ and $8x + 24$.

a Form and solve an equation in x and write down the size of all four angles.

b What sort of quadrilateral is this?

4 Form and solve an equation to find x.

a Find the size of each angle of the triangle.

b What type of triangle is this?

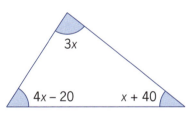

5 Catherine is solving an equation but has made an error.

> $4x + 3 = 7x + 15$
> $3x = 12$
> $x = 4$

a Show by substitution that her solution is wrong.

b Describe her error.

c Solve the equation correctly.

Brackets

You can **expand** or '**multiply out**' brackets by multiplying every term inside the bracket by the term outside.
For example, $5(x + 2) = 5x + 10$

EXAMPLE

Expand these expressions.
- **a** $4(x - 6)$
- **b** $r(r + 2)$
- **c** $a(a + b - 3c)$

Remember to multiply every term inside the bracket by the term outside.

- **a** $4x - 24$
- **b** $r^2 + 2r$
- **c** $a^2 + ab - 3ac$

r^2 means $r \times r$

- Putting expressions into brackets (the opposite of multiplying out) is called **factorising**.
For example, $9y - 6 = \mathbf{3}(3y - 2)$

Find the HCF of all the terms (in this case 3).

EXAMPLE

Factorise these expressions.
- **a** $3c - 12$
- **b** $36 - 24k$
- **c** $2m^2 + 8m$

- **a** $3c - 12$ — Look for a number (or letter) that is a factor of each term, in this case 3
  $3(\ldots - \ldots)$ Write the 3, then a set of brackets
  $3(c - 4)$ In the spaces, write in the numbers or letters that would expand to give the original expression
- **b** $12(3 - 2k)$
- **c** $2m(m + 4)$ Here, both 2 and m are factors

You can check your answer by expanding:
$3(c - 4) = 3c - 12$

You should choose the largest factor, in this case 12.

EXAMINER'S TIP
If there are 2 factors the question will normally be worth 2 marks.

When an equation has brackets, your first step could be to expand the brackets.

EXAMPLE

Solve $8(x + 5) = 3(6 - x)$.

$8(x + 5) = 3(6 - x)$
$8x + 40 = 18 - 3x$ Multiply out the brackets
$11x + 40 = 18$ Add 3x to both sides
$11x = -22$ Subtract 40 from both sides
$x = -2$ Divide both sides by 11

Exercise AA6

MEDIUM

1. Expand these expressions.
   - **a** $4(c + 5)$
   - **b** $7(y + 7)$
   - **c** $p(p - 7)$
   - **d** $y(y + z)$
   - **e** $2e(e + 5f)$
   - **f** $3f(3f - h + 5h)$

2. Factorise these expressions.
   - **a** $5h - 20$
   - **b** $28 + 7k$
   - **c** $f^2 + 9f$
   - **d** $4j + 12$
   - **e** $18d - 24$
   - **f** $40 - 60m$
   - **g** $pq - q^2$
   - **h** $3g^2 + 6g$
   - **i** $8mn + 12n^2$

3. Find and expand an expression for the area of this rectangle.

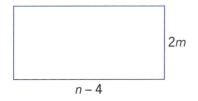

4. Solve
   - **a** $2(x + 3) = 12$
   - **b** $5(w - 1) = 20$
   - **c** $15 = 6(q + 5)$
   - **d** $4(2 - x) = -4$
   - **e** $x = 3(x - 4)$
   - **f** $3(y - 2) = 2(y + 11)$
   - **g** $6(z + 1) = 2(1 - z)$

5. Sam, Kabir and Patrick collect game cards.
   Sam has x cards, Kabir has 10 cards more than Sam and Patrick has twice as many cards as Kabir.
   Altogether they have 182 cards.
   - **a** Write an expression in terms of x for the number of cards that
     - **i** Kabir has
     - **ii** Patrick has.
   - **b** Form and solve an equation in x to find out how many cards Sam has.

6. This triangle has angles as marked.

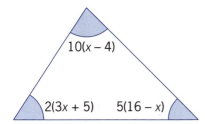

   - **a** Form and solve an equation to find x.
   - **b** Find the size of each angle of the triangle.
   - **c** What type of triangle is this?

Measures and scales

AG1

Check you understand how to read the following scales.

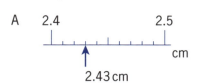

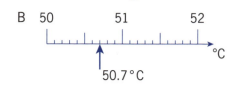

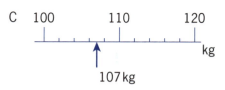

Metric system

Length
1 cm = 10 mm
1 m = 100 cm
1 m = 1000 mm
1 km = 1000 m

Mass
1 g = 1000 mg
1 kg = 1000 g
1 tonne (t) = 1000 kg

Volume and capacity
1 litre = 1000 millilitres (ml)
1 ml = 1 cm^3 (cubic cm)

Imperial system

Length
1 foot (ft) = 12 inches (in)
1 yard (y) = 3 feet

Mass
1 pound (lb) = 16 ounces (oz)
1 stone = 14 pounds

Volume and capacity
1 gallon = 8 pints

Conversion from metric to imperial units

Length
1 foot ≈ 30 cm
1 mile ≈ 1.6 km
5 miles ≈ 8 km
3 feet ≈ 1 metre

Mass
1 kg ≈ 2.2 lb
1 lb ≈ 0.5 kg

Volume and capacity
2 pints ≈ 1 litre
1 gallon ≈ 4.5 litres

Examples

1 Convert 14 m to cm.
   1 m = 100 cm
   14 m = 14 × 100 cm
   14 m = 1400 cm

2 Convert 455 mm to m.
   1 m = 1000 mm
   455 ÷ 1000 = 0.455 m

3 Convert 14 feet into yards.
   1 yard = 3 feet
   14 ÷ 3 = 4 y 2 ft

4 Convert 15 miles into km.
   5 miles ≈ 8 km
   15 miles ≈ 3 × 8 = 24

1 Convert 3260 g to kg.
   1 kg = 1000 g
   3260 ÷ 1000 = 3.26 kg

2 Convert 4.63 tonnes to kg.
   1 tonne = 1000 kg
   4.63 × 1000 = 4630 kg

3 Convert 90 000 000 g to t.
   1000 g = 1 kg
   1000 kg = 1 tonne
   90 000 000 ÷ 1000 =
   90 000 kg
   90 000 ÷ 1000 = 90 t

4 Convert 6 lb to kg.
   1 lb ≈ 0.5 kg
   6 × 0.5 = 3 kg

1 Convert 3200 cm^3 to litres.
   1 litre = 1000 cm^3
   3200 ÷ 1000 = 3.2 litres

2 Convert 9.8 litres to ml.
   1 litre = 1000 ml
   9.8 × 1000 = 9800 ml

3 Convert 19 pints to gallons.
   1 gallon = 8 pints
   19 ÷ 8 = 2.375 gallons
   or 2 gallons and 3 pints

4 Convert 5 litres to pints.
   1 litre ≈ 2 pints
   5 litres ≈ 5 × 2 = 10 pints

Exercise AG1

1 What is the reading on each scale?

   a 2   3
      |—|—|—|—|
           ↑ kg

   b 75°   80°
      |—|—|—|—|
           ↑ C

2 Which metric measures would be most appropriate to measure the following?
   a the weight of a pen
   b the length of a garden
   c the width of a TV
   d the weight of a family car
   e the capacity of a small paddling pool.

3 Which imperial measure would you use to describe
   a the volume of a swimming pool
   b the weight of a large dog
   c the distance between London and Oxford?

4 Convert the following units as specified.
   a 3 kg to g
   b 6 gallons to pints
   c 19 lb to stones and pounds
   d 35 mm to cm
   e 3.5 feet to inches
   f 102 inches to feet and inches
   g 4 m to cm
   h $2\frac{3}{4}$ stones to pounds
   i 600 ml to litres
   j 18 inches to feet

5 Find approximate metric equivalents for
   a 4 feet
   b 15 lb
   c 4 gallons
   d 12 pints

6 Find approximate imperial equivalents for
   a 200 cm
   b 25 km
   c 12 kg
   d 14 litres

7 It is about 158 miles from Swansea to Southampton. How far is this approximately in km?

8 ☆ EXAM-STYLE QUESTION ☆

> Jacob weighs $9\frac{1}{2}$ stone.
> A £1 coin weighs approximately 9.5 g.
> About how much would Jacob be worth if he were to be given his weight in pound coins?

Constructions

AG2

You can construct a triangle if you know one side and two angles.
Triangle *ABC*:
AB = 3 cm, angle *CAB* = 50°, angle *CBA* = 30°

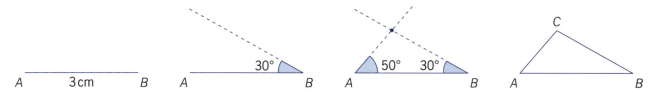

Using only a ruler and a pair of compasses you need to be able to construct:

- A triangle with three given sides

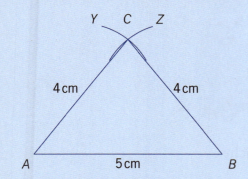

Construct a triangle with sides 5 cm, 4 cm, 4 cm.
Draw a line *AB* = 5 cm
Set compasses to 4 cm. With the compass point on *A* draw an arc *Y* above *AB*.
Keep compasses at 4 cm. With the point on *B*, draw an arc *Z* so that it intersects arc *Y* at *C*.
Join *C* to *A* and *B* to make the triangle.

- The bisector of an angle

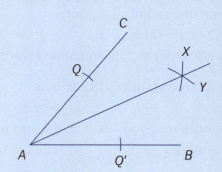

Put the compass point on *A*. Draw arcs on *AC* and *AB* at *Q* and *Q'*.
With the compass point first on *Q* and then on *Q'*, draw arcs *X* and *Y*.
Join *A* to the point where *X* and *Y* intersect.

- The perpendicular bisector of a line segment *AB*

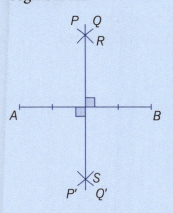

With compass point on *A*, draw arcs *P* and *P'* above and below *AB*.
Keep the same compass setting. Put the point on *B* and draw arcs *Q* and *Q'* to intersect arcs *P* and *P'* at *R* and *S*. Join *RS*.

- The perpendicular at a point on a line

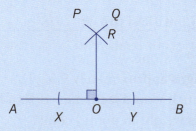

With compass point on *O*, draw arcs *X* and *Y* on *AB*.
Extend the compasses.
With compass point on *X*, then *Y*, draw arcs *P* and *Q* to intersect at *R*. Join *RO*.

- The perpendicular from a point to a line

With compass point on *T*, draw arcs *X* and *Y* on *AB*.
With compass point on *X*, then *Y*, draw arcs
P and *Q* on the opposite side of *AB* from *T*.
Draw a line joining *T* to the point of intersection of arcs
P and *Q*. Label the point *R* where this line crosses *AB*.
TR is the perpendicular from *T* to *AB*.

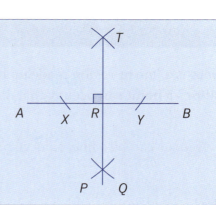

Exercise AG2

MEDIUM

1 Copy the diagrams and make them larger. Construct
   a the perpendicular bisector of line *AB*
   b the bisector of angle *AOB*.

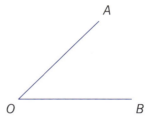

2 Copy the diagrams and construct
   a the perpendicular bisector of *AB*
   b the perpendicular from *P* to *AB*.

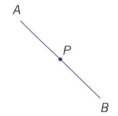

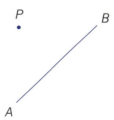

3 Construct a triangle with sides 3 cm, 4 cm and 5 cm.
   Measure all three angles of the triangle. What special sort of triangle is it?

4 Construct an equilateral triangle with sides 7 cm. Construct a perpendicular from
   the apex (top) of your triangle to the base and measure the length of this perpendicular.

5 Construct a triangle *ABC* with *CB* = 7.4 cm, angle *C* = 60°
   and angle *B* = 48°. Measure the size of the third angle.

6 Using a protractor, draw accurately an angle of 70°.
   Bisect your angle and check your accuracy by measuring.

7 Construct an isosceles triangle *ABC* with base *BC* = 11 cm and base angles of 50°.
   a Bisect angle *BAC*.
   b Bisect the side *AB*.

8 Line *AB* is 10 cm long. Without using a protractor, construct
   the triangle *APB* in which angle *BAP* = 60° and angle *PBA* = 30°.

9 Construct an equilateral triangle *PQR* with sides 9 cm. From each
   vertex of the triangle construct a perpendicular to the opposite side.
   These lines are called altitudes of the triangle. If your construction
   is accurate these three altitudes will intersect at a common point.

Loci

AG3

A **locus** is a line or region made up of all the possible positions a point can occupy that obey a certain rule.

- A locus can be a line, a curve or a region.

The locus of a point which is a constant distance, 3 cm, from a fixed point O is a **circle** of radius 3 cm.

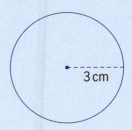

The locus of a point which is equidistant from two fixed points A and B is the **perpendicular bisector** of the line segment joining A to B.

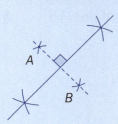

The locus of a point which is a constant distance d from a fixed line is a pair of **parallel lines**.

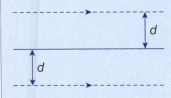

The locus of a point which is equidistant from two lines OA and OB is the **angle bisector** AOB.

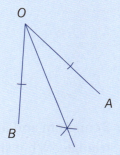

EXAMPLE

Draw the locus of points which are less than 3 cm from the line segment AB.

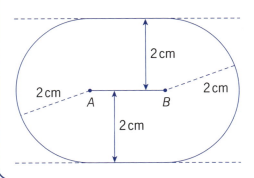

To draw the locus from points A and B, set a compass to 2 cm and draw a semicircle at each end of the line.

Exercise AG3

MEDIUM

1 Copy the diagram and make it larger. Construct these loci.

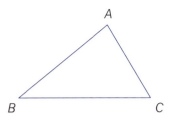

- **a** The locus of point P which is always 2 cm from B.
- **b** The locus of point R which is equidistant from the line segments AB and AC and is inside the triangle ABC.
- **c** The locus of point Q which is equidistant from points A and C.

2 WX, XY, YZ and ZW are hedges surrounding a field.
Copy the diagram and sketch and describe the following loci.

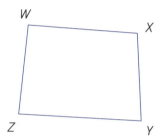

- **a** The locus of a football that is kicked so that it is always the same distance from X as from Z.
- **b** The locus of a sheep which moves from the hedge ZY to the corner W so that it remains equidistant from WX and WZ.

3 Two villages, A and B, are 20 km apart. B is due south of A.
The fire brigade from village A looks after a region 10 km around A while the fire brigade from village B looks after a region 12 km around B. Using a scale of 1 cm for 4 km, draw a diagram to show the region covered by both fire brigades.

4 A guard dog is on a leash 6 m long. The leash is attached to the corner of a building as shown.

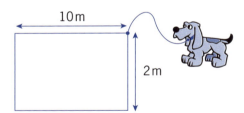

- **a** Copy the diagram and sketch the region which the dog can guard.
- **b** Draw two more diagrams to show the regions the dog can guard if the leash is
  - **i** 9 m long
  - **ii** 11 m long.

Loci

Scale drawing

AG4

You need to be able to measure both lengths and angles accurately. Check your skills by measuring the lengths and angles below (you may need to extend the angle lines).

A
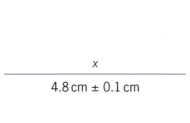
4.8 cm ± 0.1 cm

B
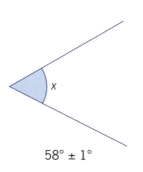
58° ± 1°

C

150° ± 1°

D

324° ± 1°

Measure acute angle and subtract from 360°.

The key to understanding a scale drawing is to clearly understand the scale being used.

EXAMPLE

Suppose in a scale drawing 1 cm represents 4 km.
a What distance would 3.6 cm represent?
b What length on the scale drawing would represent 18 km?

....

a 3.6 cm represents 3.6 × 4 = 14.4 km
b 18 km is represented by 18 × 4 = 4.5 cm

EXAMPLE

John hits a golf ball from the tee to A, then to B and then to C.
How far in total has he hit the ball? How much further does he need to hit it to get it in the hole?

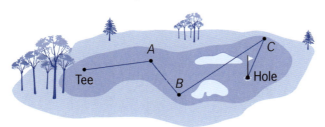

Map scale 1 cm = 36 m

....

TEE ⟶ A ~ 1.8 cm = 1.8 × 60 = 108 m
A ⟶ B ~ 1.2 cm = 1.2 × 60 = 72 m
B ⟶ C ~ 2.8 cm = 2.8 × 60 = 168 m

Therefore he has hit the ball
108 + 72 + 168 = 348 m
The distance from C to the hole is approximately:
1.2 cm = 1.2 × 60 = 72 m

Scale drawing

EXAMPLE

Produce an accurate scale drawing of the journey shown in the diagram.

Use a scale of 1 cm = 1 km.
What is the direct distance from A to D?

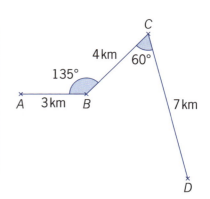

Direct distance from A to D = 8.9 cm = 8.9 km

Exercise AG4

MEDIUM LOW

1   Measure the following angles and lengths as accurately as you can.

   a 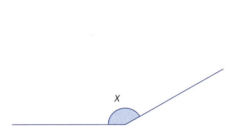   b 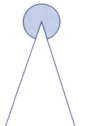   c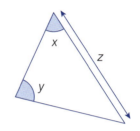

2   Produce a scale drawing of the following using a scale of 1 cm for 1 km. Find the direct distance from the starting point A to the finishing point D.

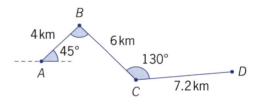

3   A farmer wants to make a scale drawing of the fields that make up his farm. He made this sketch.

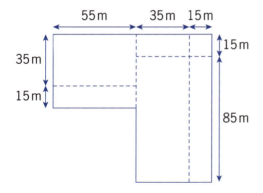

Make an accurate scale drawing of his fields using a scale of 1 cm to represent 20 m.

4   This map of an island has a scale of 5 cm represents 8 km. Jocelyn has to drive from A to D then from D to C and then from C to B. If diesel costs £1.15 per litre and her van does 36 km for every 4 litres of diesel, how much does her journey cost?

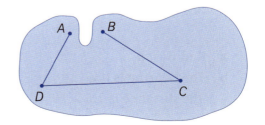

Scale drawing   37

Maps and bearings

This diagram shows the key points of the compass.

The key word in a bearing statement is **from**. The bearing of *B* from *A* tells you that the North line is drawn at *A* while the bearing of *A* from *B* tells you that the North line has to be drawn at *B*.

Here are some examples of bearings. You should check them by measuring the bearings yourself.

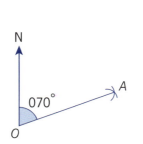 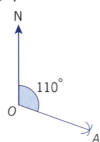 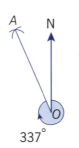

Bearings are always 3-digit numbers, for example 080°

EXAMPLE

On what bearing are you travelling when you go

a North   b South   c South-West?

....

a 000°   b 180°   c 225°

EXAMPLE

If Suzi travels on a bearing of 315° for 8 km starting at her house, show on a scale drawing her position relative to her house. Use a scale of 1 cm for 2 km.

If you do a rough sketch first this will help you get an idea of how much space you need for your drawing.

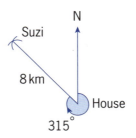

EXAMPLE

On this map the scale is 1 cm = 10 km
a Which beach is on a bearing of about 230° from the airport?
b Find the bearing and distance of the village from Six Hill.

....

a Red Beach
b The bearing is 035°
   The distance is 1.5 × 10 = 15 km

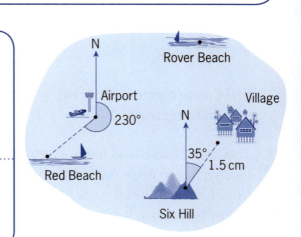

Maps and bearings

EXAMPLE

Using a scale of 1 cm for 1 km, make a scale drawing of the following journey.
Susanne walks 7 km from X to Y on a bearing of 130°.
She then walks 6 km from Y to Z on a bearing of 210°.
She then walks directly from Z back to X.
How far has she walked in total and on what bearing does she travel to get from Z to X?

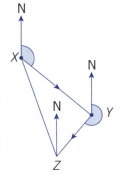

> Do a rough sketch first to get an idea of how the journey looks, then do an accurate scale drawing

Bearing is approximately 360 − 12 = 348°
and distance is 5 cm = 5 km

Exercise AG5

MEDIUM LOW

1 Using a protractor, measure the bearing of B from A in these diagrams.

a 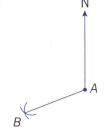   b 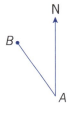   c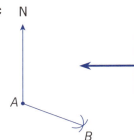

> You will need to trace these angles and extend the arms so that you can measure the angles.

2 Which compass directions correspond to the following bearings?
  a 270°   b 045°   c 315°

3 A ship sails on a bearing of 200° for 20 km until it reaches its destination.
  a Construct a scale drawing to show its journey.
  b If the ship returns on the same route, on what bearing does it travel?

4 a Describe the journey which begins at A and finishes at C in terms of the distance travelled and bearings.
  b By scale drawing, find the direct distance of C from A.

5 a Mike was out walking when he sprained his ankle and had to call for help. He was able to say that the village was on a bearing of 050° and that Six Hill was on a bearing of 135°. Copy the diagram in the third example above and use it to locate Mike.
  b What is Mike's bearing from the airport?

Maps and bearings

Pythagoras' theorem

AG6

Pythagoras' theorem describes the relationship between the lengths of the sides of a **right-angled** triangle.

The longest side of a right-angled triangle is called the **hypotenuse**.

- $a^2 + b^2 = c^2$ or $c^2 = a^2 + b^2$

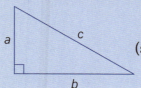

(short side)² + (short side)² = (hypotenuse)²

Pythagoras' theorem allows you to find one side of a right-angled triangle if you know the other two sides.

EXAMPLE

Find the length x in these triangles. Give your answers to 3 sf.

a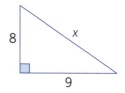

b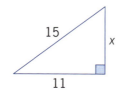

When you have to find one of the shorter sides you have to do a subtraction.

a The missing side is the hypotenuse.
$x^2 = 9^2 + 8^2$
$= 81 + 64$
$= 145$
$x = \sqrt{145} = 12.0$ cm (3 sf)

b This time a shorter side is missing.
$15^2 = x^2 + 11^2$
$x^2 = 15^2 - 11^2$
$= 225 - 121$
$= 104$
$x = \sqrt{104} = 10.2$ cm (3 sf)

Do not round until the final answer.
Write units in your final answer.

EXAMPLE

a A helicopter flies 24 km west and then 18 km north. How far is the helicopter from its starting position?

b Find the length of the diagonal of a square of side length 12 mm. Give your answer to 3 significant figures.

a Draw a sketch and identify which side is missing.

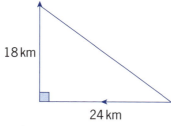

b Draw the square and label the diagonal x.

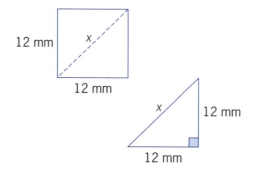

$x^2 = 24^2 + 18^2 = 900$
$x = \sqrt{900} = 30$ km

$x^2 = 12^2 + 12^2 = 288$
$x = \sqrt{288} = 17.0$ mm (3 sf)

Two well-known right-angled triangles are the 3, 4, 5 triangle and the 5, 12, 13 triangle. Any enlargements of these triangles will also be right-angled, for example 6, 8, 10 or 15, 36, 39 etc.

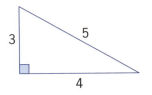
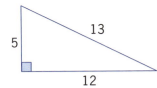

Exercise AG6

MEDIUM

1 Find the missing sides in these triangles (give your answers to 3 sf).

a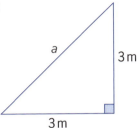
b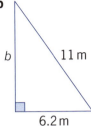
c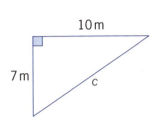
d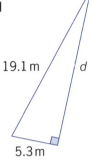

2 Janet puts some wire fencing around this triangular garden. She uses 5 m for the shorter side and 12 m for the longest side.
What is the total length of wire that she uses?

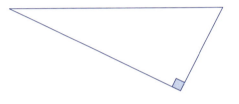

3 Mark walks 400 m east and then 250 m south.
How far is Mark from his starting point?

4 A and B have coordinates (1, 1) and (5, 4) respectively.
 a What is the length of AC?
 b What is the length of BC?
 c Calculate the length of AB.

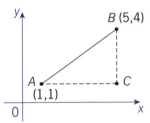

5 Find the length x in this diagram.

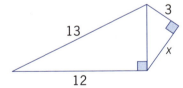

6 A sail has the shape shown in the diagram. Reinforcing tape is put around its edges.
 a Assuming the sail is approximately a right-angled triangle, how much tape is needed in total?
 b If the tape costs 87 pence per metre, what will be the cost (answer in £ p).

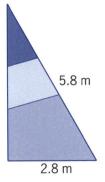

7 Do you think 7 cm, 17 cm and 15 cm could be the lengths of the sides of a right-angled triangle? Explain your answer carefully.

Collecting and handling data — AS1

- **Primary** data is data that you collect yourself. You can collect data by conducting a **survey** or an **experiment**.
- **Secondary** data is data taken from an existing source such as newspapers or the internet.
- Data can be **discrete** or **continuous**.
- A **two-way table** shows two sets of data about the same group of people or things, for example, hair colour and eye colour.

You can count discrete data, for example the number of eggs in a nest. Continuous data is data you measure, for example weight, height.

		Hair colour			
		Blue	Brown	Red	Black
Eye colour	Blue				
	Grey				
	Green				
	Brown				

If the group you are surveying is small you can collect data from everyone, but if the group is large you need to choose a **sample**.

- To choose a **random sample**, you can assign a number to each possible member of the sample and use a random number generator to pick numbers.
- **Questionnaires** should be relevant and useful to your survey.

Use clear language. Cover all options and leave no gaps between the answer choices.

You have to ensure that the sample is not biased. **Bias** can arise if, for example, you only ask your friends or you only ask people in a certain age group.
In general, the larger the sample size the more reliable is the data.

EXAMPLE

Wendy carried out a survey to find out how much people spent on food each week. She asked 100 people at the supermarket closest to where she lives on a Tuesday morning. Explain why Wendy's survey might be biased and advise her on how to avoid this bias.

Only asking shoppers at one supermarket – she should ask shoppers at all supermarkets.
Only asking shoppers who shop at a store – she should include people who shop online.
Only asking shoppers on one weekday – she should ask on other days including weekends.
Only asking shoppers at one time of day – she should vary the time of day when she carries out the survey.

EXAMPLE

This question appeared in a survey about time spent using a mobile phone.

How much time do you spend on your mobile phone?
Less then 5 minutes ☐   Up to 10 minutes ☐   Over an hour ☐

Criticise the question, and write a better question.

The question does not have a time frame.
It does not specify just phone calls or also using the phone to listen to music or play games.
The answer choices have gaps and overlaps.
How long, on average, do you spend making calls on your mobile each day?
Less than 10 minutes ☐   10–30 minutes ☐   Over 30 minutes ☐

Exercise AS1

MEDIUM

1. Terry began drawing this observation sheet to collect data on women's shoe sizes and glove sizes.

	Shoe size				
Glove size					

   One manufacturer makes women's shoes in sizes that range from 3 to 8 and gloves in sizes that range from extra small to large.
   a   Copy the observation sheet and put the sizes on it.
   b   In Terry's survey   7 people had shoe size 5 and glove size medium
                                    9 people had shoe size 4 and glove size small.
       Add this information to your observation sheet.

2. Design an observation sheet to collect data on colour and type of vehicle in a road traffic survey. You will need to choose categories for the different types of vehicle.

3. Answers to a crossword puzzle are completed either across or down. In a crossword puzzle book all the crosswords have across answers 4 to 9 letters long and down answers 5 to 10 letters long.
   a   i   Design an observation sheet to capture data about the length of answers in this crossword book.
       ii 12 crosswords had across answers 7 letters long and down answers 6 letters long.
           Write this value in the correct position of your observation sheet.
   b   Debbie wants to do a survey of the crosswords in the book. She gives each of twelve colleagues a copy of the crossword book and a questionnaire to complete.
       Give two reasons why Debbie's survey may be biased.

4. Below are the questions used in a survey on hair products. Some of the questions are not suitable.
   Write what is wrong with them and write better questions.
   a   What colour is your hair?   Blonde   Brown   Black
   b   Is your hair dyed?   Yes   No
   c   How long is your hair?   Short   Medium   Long
   d   How many times per week do you wash your hair?
       Once   Twice   Every day
   e   Do you always use conditioner?   Yes   No   Sometimes

Collecting and handling data   43

Averages and range

AS2

- The **range** of a data set = largest value – smallest value
- An **average** is a representative value of a set of data.
- The **mode** is the data value that occurs most often. ← A data set can have no mode, one mode or more than one mode.
- The **median** is the middle value when data are arranged in order.
  If there are two middle numbers, the median is the middle value of these two numbers. For example, for the data set
  $$2 \quad 2 \quad 4 \quad 5 \quad 7 \quad 8 \quad 10 \quad 11$$
  the middle values are 5 and 7, so the median is 6.
- The **mean** is calculated by adding all the data values then dividing by the number of pieces of data.

You can use the measures range, mode, median and mean to compare data sets.
When comparing data sets, always compare the same type of measure, for example mean with mean, not mean with mode.

EXAMPLE

These are the monthly allowances for a group of students:
£27   £34   £24   £10   £15   £12   £30   £16

a Work out the
  i mode   **ii** median   **iii** mean   **iv** range
b Another student's pocket money is £27. If this amount is included, how would it affect the measures calculated in part **a**?

---

a i There is no mode.
  ii In order   £10   £12   £15   £16   £24   £27   £30   £34
     Two middle values £16 and £24, so median = £20
  iii Total 27 + 34 + 24 + 10 + 15 + 12 + 30 + 16 = £168
       168 ÷ 8 = 21   Mean = £21
  iv Range 34 – 10 = £24
b £27 is greater than mean and median so both of these will increase.
  There will be two amounts of £27, so £27 is now the mode.
  The range is unchanged as £27 lies between the highest and lowest amounts.

- A **stem-and-leaf diagram** displays all the data in a small data set.
  ▸ The stem is written on one side of a vertical line, with the leaves on the other side.
  ▸ Leaves are written in order, smallest next to the stem.
  ▸ Always write a key.

```
3 | 5  6  8  9
4 | 1  1  1  2  2  4  6  8
5 | 1  2  2  3  5  8
6 | 1  2  3
```
Key: 3|5 means 35 hours

> **EXAMPLE**
>
> The times taken, in seconds, for 19 children to complete a jigsaw are
>
> 69 103 94 65 88 76 78 93 105 112 83 98 85 89 91 76 87 90 82
>
> **a** Draw a stem-and-leaf diagram to display these data.
> **b** Write **i** the median **ii** the range.
>
> ---
>
> **a**
> 11 | 2
> 10 | 3 5
> 9 | 0 1 3 4 8
> 8 | 2 3 5 7 8 9
> 7 | 6 6 8
> 6 | 5 9   Key: 8 | 2 means 82 seconds
>
> *Use tens as the stem and units as the leaves. 112 is 11 tens and 2 units. Choose any value in the diagram for the key.*
>
> **b i** Median $\frac{1}{2}(19+1)$th = 10th value, median = 88 seconds
>
> **ii** Range = 112 − 65 = 47 seconds

Exercise AS2

MEDIUM LOW

1 Gemma has a spelling test each week. The spelling tests are always scored out of the same total. Her scores for fifteen consecutive weeks are

18 13 15 16 17 16 9 12 7 11 20 19 6 12 14

a One week Gemma scored full marks on her spelling test. What is the total possible score for the spelling tests each week?
b What is the range of Gemma's scores?
c Work out the score that is
  i the mode **ii** the median **iii** the mean
d In week sixteen Gemma scored 19. When this score is included what is her new
  i mode **ii** median **iii** mean?

2 The table shows the scores of a multiplication test and a division test taken by a group of ten students. There were the same number of questions in each test.

Multiplication	25	18	20	20	16	12	14	20	23	9
Division	22	19	13	22	14	15	15	19	19	12

Were the students better at multiplication or division?
You must justify your answer with calculations, explaining how they help you decide.

3 These are the times taken, to the nearest minute, to deliver leaflets to 15 roads.

22 15 28 34 29 9 11 24 23 16 20 30 31 32 41

a Work out the mean delivery time.
b Represent these data on a stem-and-leaf diagram.

Finding averages from tables   AS3

You can summarise large amounts of raw data in a table to show the frequencies.

Shoe size	3	4	5	6
Frequency	2	39	36	13

Mode is 4   Median is 5

> You use the frequencies to find the various averages. Do not use frequencies as averages.

EXAMPLE

On a box of drawing pins the average contents are stated as 50. The table shows the number of drawing pins in 35 boxes.

Drawing pins	48	49	50	51	52	53	54
Frequency	3	6	21	1	2	1	1

Joni says that the average is 50, whatever measure of average is used. Explain why Joni is correct.

Mode is 50 as 50 has the highest frequency (21).
35 boxes, middle value is $\frac{1}{2}(35 + 1) = $ 18th value, $3 + 6 = 9$, $9 + 21 = 30$
The 18th value is 50, so median = 50
Total number of pins $= 48 \times 3 + 49 \times 6 + 50 \times 21 + 51 + 52 \times 2 + 53 + 54$
$= 1750$
mean $= 1750 \div 35 = 50$
All three averages are 50, so Joni is correct.

> To find the median in a small data set, find the $\frac{1}{2}(n + 1)$th value. Imagine listing the number of pins in order. 50 would be the 18th number in the list.

You can group data when there are lots of different values.

- In grouped data
  - The **modal class** is the class with the highest frequency.
  - You can find the class in which the **median** lies, not an actual median value.
  - You calculate an **estimated mean** using the midpoint and the frequency of each class.

EXAMPLE

The table summarises the number of miles Reuben cycled each day for the first 29 days in April.

Miles cycled (m)	$0 \leq m < 20$	$20 \leq m < 40$	$40 \leq m < 60$	$60 \leq m < 80$
Frequency	5	9	11	4

a Work out an estimate of the mean number of miles Reuben cycled.
b How many miles could Reuben cycle on April 30th so that the class interval in which the median lies does not change? Explain your answer.

> Estimate does not mean guess – use the midpoint and the frequency of each class. Remember to divide by the total frequency, not the number of classes.

a Total miles $10 \times 5 + 30 \times 9 + 50 \times 11 + 70 \times 4 = 1150$
$1150 \div 29 = 39.655…$ mean = 39.7 miles

b $\frac{1}{2}(29 + 1) = $ 15th value $5 + 9 = 14$, so the median (15th value) is in the class $40 \leq m < 60$
With 30 values median will be $\frac{1}{2}(30 + 1) = $ 15.5th value, so you average the 15th and 16th values. Both must be in the $40 \leq m < 60$ class for the median to stay where it is.
So on April 30th Reuben must cycle a distance of 40 miles or more.

46 Finding averages from tables

Exercise AS3

MEDIUM

1 Henry drew this table to show the number of tracks on each of the CDs he owned.

Number of tracks	7	8	9	10	11
Number of CDs	4	6	12	5	2

   a Write
      i   the median   ii   the modal number of tracks.
   b Work out the mean number of tracks.

2 The numbers and prices of theatre tickets available for a performance are shown in the table.

Ticket price, £	50	40	25	15
Number available	140	50	200	10

   a Calculate the mean price of a theatre ticket.
   b For a special performance one evening all ticket prices were reduced by £5.
      What was the mean price of a theatre ticket for that performance?

3 The number of hats of different sizes sold by a department store is given in the table.

Hat size	$6\frac{3}{8}$	$6\frac{1}{2}$	$6\frac{5}{8}$	$6\frac{3}{4}$	$6\frac{7}{8}$	7	$7\frac{1}{8}$	$7\frac{1}{4}$	$7\frac{3}{8}$	$7\frac{1}{2}$	$7\frac{5}{8}$
Number sold	1	0	2	3	8	15	12	3	0	0	0

When the manager of the store orders new hats to sell, which type of average should he use? Give reasons for your answer and show your calculations.

4 The table shows the times a sample of 84 students spent doing homework one evening.

Time, m minutes	$0 < m \leq 20$	$20 < m \leq 40$	$40 < m \leq 60$	$60 < m \leq 80$	$80 < m \leq 100$	$100 < m \leq 120$
Frequency	1	21	11	22	8	21

   a Work out an estimate of the mean time.
   b Which class contains the median?
   c Explain why the modal class may not be a good measure of average to use with these data.

5 Ahmed recorded the number of hours of sunshine in May and June.

May

Number of hours of sunshine, h	Number of days
$0 \leq h < 2$	5
$2 \leq h < 4$	14
$4 \leq h < 6$	7
$6 \leq h < 8$	5

June

Number of hours of sunshine, h	Number of days
$0 \leq h < 2$	5
$2 \leq h < 4$	7
$4 \leq h < 6$	10
$6 \leq h < 8$	8

   a Calculate estimates of the mean number of hours of sunshine in May and in June.
   b Write   i the class which contains the median   ii the modal class   for both May and June.

Finding averages from tables

Pie charts and bar charts

AS4

You can use a **pie chart** to represent non-numerical data (like flavours and colours).
- A pie chart is a circle shared out between the frequencies – the bigger the frequency the larger the share.
  The **mode** has the largest share.
- To draw a pie chart, work out 360° ÷ total frequency, multiply this answer by the frequency of each class to find its share of the pie.
• A **bar chart** represents **discrete** data and can be used for data given in categories.
  - All bars are rectangles of the same width with gaps between the bars.
  - The height of each bar represents the frequency.
  - The mode is the highest bar.

EXAMPLE

The number of ASBOs, to the nearest 100, issued each year from 2003 to 2008 are given in the table.

Year	2003	2004	2005	2006	2007	2008
ASBOs	1300	3500	4100	2700	2300	2000

Draw a bar chart to represent these data.

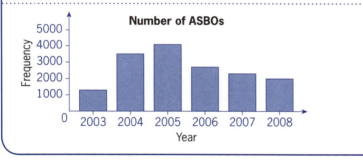

An ASBO is an Anti-social Behaviour Order, which is issued by courts in the UK for minor offences.

EXAMPLE

This bar chart shows the estimated maximum Internet download speeds in megabytes per second in Great Britain in May 2010.
Draw a pie chart for these data.

Total download speeds 5.4 + 5.0 + 4.8 + 4.8 = 20
360 ÷ 20 = 18°
England   5.4 × 18 = 97.2°
Scotland   5.0 × 18 = 90.0°
Wales   4.8 × 18 = 86.4°
N. Ireland 4.8 × 18 = 86.4°
Check   Total   360°

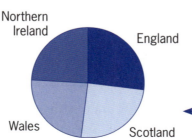

Label each sector or use a key.
The pie chart must cover the whole circle.
Check that your angles add up to 360°.

Exercise AS4

1. The owner of a beach café drew this table to show the number and type of drinks he sold one day in August.

Tea	Coffee	Water	Fizzy drink	Still drink
80	64	160	40	16

Draw a bar chart to display the information.

2. The bar chart shows the number of books in a school library for some subjects.

   a How many more books are there for physics than DT?
   b How many books are there altogether?
   c Which subject is the mode?

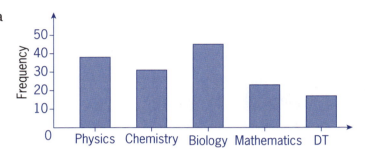

3. The results of a poll in June 2010 on voting intentions are given in this pie chart.

   a What angle is represented by 'Others'?
   b If 1000 people voted according to the results of this poll, how many would vote Labour?

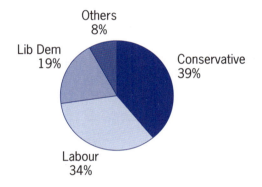

4. Avenue School students live in five local villages. This bar chart shows the number of students attending the school from each village in January 2010.

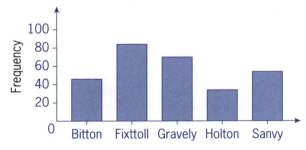

   a How many students came from Sanvy village?
   b How many students are there at Avenue School?
   c Draw a pie chart to show the same information as the bar chart.

Histograms and frequency polygons — AS5

- Histograms and frequency polygons are both **frequency diagrams** that are used to display **grouped** continuous data.
- A **histogram** has bars to represent the frequencies.
  - There are no gaps between the bars.
  - Both axes have a scale.

EXAMPLE

The table summarises the number of miles Reuben cycled each day in July.

Miles cycled (m)	0 ≤ m < 20	20 ≤ m < 40	40 ≤ m < 60	60 ≤ m < 80
Frequency	4	9	13	5

Draw a histogram for these data.

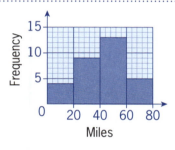

This is an **equal-interval histogram**. The bars are all the same width.

- A **frequency polygon** has straight lines joining the midpoints of each class interval.

You can use a histogram to draw a frequency polygon. Just join the midpoints of the tops of each bar.

When you use graphs to compare data sets, you should always make comparisons between the same type of average (compare means or medians or modes) and the range.

EXAMPLE

Compare the profits (or losses) for these samples of retailers and manufacturers.

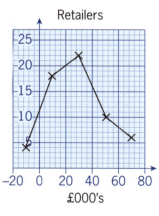
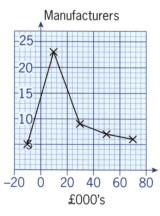

Don't be tempted to compare individual values such as the last class of both graphs.

Don't be tempted to compare the height of the peak. Compare the classes of the highest peak from each graph.

On average, retailers made more profit as their modal class (£20 000–£40 000) is higher than the modal class (£0–£20 000) for manufacturers.

Exercise AS5

1. These are the times, in minutes, that a group of students spent using a computer one evening.

Time, m minutes	$0 < m \leq 20$	$20 < m \leq 40$	$40 < m \leq 60$	$60 < m \leq 80$	$80 < m \leq 100$	$100 < m \leq 120$
Frequency	5	11	17	15	13	8

   a Draw a histogram to display these data.
   b Draw a frequency polygon to display these data.
   c What is the modal class interval?

2. Todd measured the lengths of leaves, in mm, dropped from trees in his garden one day in autumn.

   44 85 72 42 37 29 78 43 79 91 43
   45 28 42 79 34 92 87 41 43 43 78
   82 47 85 43 92 32 86 76

   a Copy and complete the tally chart for these data.

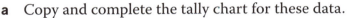

Leaf length, l mm	Tally	Frequency
$20 < l \leq 30$		
$30 < l \leq 40$		
$40 < l \leq 50$		
$50 < l \leq 60$		
$60 < l \leq 70$		
$70 < l \leq 80$		
$80 < l \leq 90$		
$90 < l \leq 100$		

   Remember:
   A tally chart collects data in groups of 5 like this ||||

   b Draw a histogram to show the length of the leaves.
   c Explain how the data suggest that there may be more than one type of tree in Todd's garden.

3. In a triathlon there are transition times when competitors change sport from swim to bike and then from bike to run. Paolo collected data on the transition times, in seconds, for 80 competitors. These are the transition times for swim to bike.

Time, s seconds	$120 < s \leq 150$	$150 < s \leq 180$	$180 < s \leq 210$	$210 < s \leq 240$	$240 < s \leq 270$
Frequency	12	21	26	15	6

   a Draw a frequency polygon to represent these data.
   b Paolo drew this frequency polygon for the transition times for bike to run.
   Compare the transition times taken for swim to bike and for bike to run.

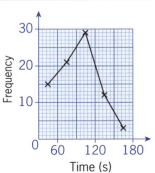

Histograms and frequency polygons

Arithmetic with integers and decimals — BN1

You should be able to add and subtract integers and decimals without using a calculator.

LOOK BACK
See Topic AN1 to revise multiplying and dividing by a negative number

EXAMPLE

Calculate
- **a** $12.3 + 0.04 + 5.1$
- **b** $5.6 + 9 + 1.54$
- **c** $12 - 4.5$
- **d** $6.3 - 4.16$

After every **whole number** there is an invisible decimal point.

```
a    12.3        b     5.6       c    12.0       d    6.30
      0.04             9.0           - 4.5           - 4.16
    + 5.1           + 1.54            7.5             2.14
    17.44            16.14
```

Remember to line up the hundreds and tens and put a 0 after the decimal point if needed.

EXAMPLE

Colin works out $4.1 + 12$ like this:

```
  4.1
+ 1 2
  5.3
```

Explain what he has done wrong and work out the correct answer.

Colin forgot the decimal point after the 12 and got the numbers out of line.
```
   4.1
 +12.0
  16.1
```

It is important to always line up the decimal points in a single column.

You can use place value facts to multiply and divide.

EXAMPLE

- **a** Given that $3 \times 7 = 21$, find
  - **i** 0.3×700
  - **ii** $210 \div 0.7$
- **b** Calculate
  - **i** 3.1×0.6
  - **ii** $45 \div 0.3$
  - **iii** $0.015 \div 0.05$

---

a i $0.3 = 3 \div 10$ and $700 = 7 \times 100$
So $0.3 \times 700 = 21 \div 10 \times 100 = 210$

ii $210 = 21 \times 10$ and $0.7 = 7 \div 10$
So $210 \div 0.7 = 3 \times 10 \times 10 = 300$

b i
```
   31
  ×6
  186
```

Check the answer is sensible. 0.6 is a bit more than "half", and half of 3 is 1.5. This answer is a bit bigger than 1.5 ✓

So $3.1 \times 0.6 = 1.86$ Count how many digits are after the decimal point. There should be the same number of digits in the answer as in the calculation.

ii $45 \div 0.3 = 450 \div 3 = 150$
Move the decimal point in both numbers until the divisor is a whole number.

The point moves right 1 place in each number.

iii $0.015 \div 0.05 = 1.5 \div 5$
$0.015 \div 0.05 = 0.3$

```
    0.3
  5)1.5
```

The point in the answer is **above** the point in the question.

Exercise BN1

LOW

1 Calculate:
   - a 12.3 + 1.6
   - b 10.7 − 3.6
   - c 2.4 + 1.39 + 0.97
   - d 8 − 1.9
   - e 14 + 1.2
   - f 7.3 − 2.66
   - g 2.7 + 0.36 − 1.8
   - h 4.2 − 1.04 + 7
   - i 2.08 + 32 − 0.82

   A calculator must not be used in this exercise.

2 Calculate:
   - a 12.3 × 4
   - b 2.7 × 5
   - c 9.04 ÷ 2
   - d 1.25 × 0.5
   - e 4.4 ÷ 0.2
   - f 12.64 ÷ 0.4
   - g 13 × 1.2
   - h 240 ÷ 0.6
   - i 121 ÷ 1.1
   - j 68.7 ÷ 0.3
   - k 7.4 × 0.04
   - l 3.8 × 2.1

3 15 × 18 = 270.
   Use this fact to work out each answer.
   - a 1.5 × 1.8
   - b 27 ÷ 18
   - c 1.5 × 18
   - d 270 ÷ 18
   - e 2700 ÷ 18

4 Ian's car will travel an average of 35 miles on one gallon of fuel.
   How far will it travel on 0.4 gallons of fuel?

5 A serving of cereal contains 3.1 milligrams of iron.
   Rhoda has one serving of cereal a day.
   How many milligrams of iron does she get from this cereal in a week?

6 Hamid writes down the number of kilometres he drives each day.

Mon	Tue	Wed	Thu	Fri	Sat	Sun
25	4.6	13.8	102.6	58.9	16.6	48.1

   - a How many km did he drive in the week?
   - b How many km longer is his longest drive than his shortest drive?
   - c On Wednesday he made three short drives.
        On average, how long was each drive?

7 This pentagon has every side the same length.
   The distance all around it is 28.5 cm.
   How long is one side?

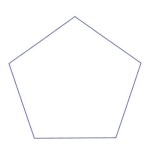

Not to scale

8 Ethan's electricity bill is £36.80.
   Each unit of electricity costs £0.80.
   How many units did Ethan use?

Arithmetic with integers and decimals

Estimating and checking decimal calculations — BN2

You can **estimate** answers to decimal calculations like 14.82 ÷ 2.97:

- Round the numbers **in your head**.   = 15 ÷ 3
- Work out the answer, writing down what you do. = 5
- Does the answer look sensible?   ✓

← **LOOK BACK**
See Topic AN3 to revise rounding.

You can also **check** answers to problems that have already been worked out, using one of these techniques:

- Work the problem out backwards using **inverse operations**.
- Work out the problem using simple, round numbers.
- Just check that the answer is sensible.

EXAMPLE

Find the answers that are clearly wrong.
a 12.39 ÷ 5.82 = 6.57
b 2.186 + 15.3 = 17.486
c $\dfrac{5.18^2}{1.2 + 3.9} = 26.26$

---

a 12.39 ÷ 5.82 = 6.57
   This is roughly 12 ÷ 6 = 2 so 6.57 ✗
b 2.186 + 15.3 = 17.486
   This is roughly 2 + 15 = 17 so 17.486 is probable ✓
c $\dfrac{5.18^2}{1.2 + 3.9} = 26.26$
   This is roughly $\dfrac{5^2}{1+4} = \dfrac{25}{5} = 5$ so 26.26 ✗

These have been worked out by rounding each number to the nearest whole number.

EXAMPLE

Check these calculations.
a 21.6 ÷ 3 = 7.2
b $\sqrt{8.1} = 0.9$

---

a 21.6 ÷ 3 = 7.2   The inverse calculation is 7.2 × 3
                     = 21.6 ✓
b $\sqrt{8.1} = 0.9$ The inverse is 0.9^2 or 0.9 × 0.9
                         = 0.81 ✗

(0.9 × 0.9 is the same as 9 × 9 with 2 decimal places put in)

Exercise BN2

MEDIUM

A calculator must not be used in this exercise.

1. Find the answers that are clearly wrong. Show your working.
   - a 12.38 − 1.7 = 12.26
   - b 9.25 × 2.1 = 19.425
   - c 16.2 + 9.09 − 4 = 10.67
   - d 1.2^2 = 14.4
   - e $\sqrt{1.69}$ = 1.3
   - f 10.46 × 2.1 − 13.45 = 8.516

2. Show how you can check these calculations.
   - a 15.3 − 2.7 = 12.6
   - b 71.3 + 5.12 = 76.42
   - c 0.25 × 5 = 1.25
   - d 20.5 ÷ 5 = 4.1
   - e (4.03 + 1.97) ÷ 6 = 1
   - f 3.2 × 1.5 − 2.2 = 2.6

3. Work out an approximate answer to each calculation. Show your working.
   - a 13.78 ÷ 2.33
   - b 45.7 × 11.3
   - c 15.823 − 3.71
   - d (106.3 + 4.9) ÷ 11.3
   - e $5.6 \times \sqrt{17.1}$
   - f $11.78^2 - 14.2$

4. a Rewrite this with each number rounded to the nearest whole number.

   $$\frac{13.9 + 8.09}{15.23 - 9.8}$$

   b Work out an approximate value for the calculation.

5. Sally pays £0.245 for each unit of electricity. In a month she uses 108 units of electricity. Work out an estimate of how much Sally's electricity bill will be for the month. Don't forget to add VAT at 5%.

ELECTRICITY BILLING DETAIL

Kingston Electricity Distribution Limited is the Licensed Distributor and provider of standard supply service: Utilities Kingston is an affiliate providing billing services)

Mr. and Mrs. Smith
14, King Street
London

Reading last time	Reading this time	Tariff	Units	Price of each unit	Amount
13467	13575	Unrestricted units	108	£0.245	xxxxx
		Monthly Direct Debit Discount			
		Vat at 5% on charges of XXXX			xxx
		Total this Invoice			xxxxx

Estimating and checking decimal calculations

Terminating and recurring decimals BN3

- **Terminating decimals** have a fixed number of digits.

  0.12 and 1.255 and 3.3333 are terminating decimals.

You can write a terminating decimal as a fraction:

- Find the value of the column containing the last decimal digit.
- This is the denominator of the fraction.
- Write the fraction with the decimal digits (after the decimal point) as the numerator.
- Cancel your fraction where possible.

U	.	$\frac{1}{10}$	$\frac{1}{100}$	$\frac{1}{1000}$	$\frac{1}{10000}$
0	.	1	2		

$0.12 = \frac{12}{100} = \frac{3}{25}$

- **Recurring decimals** have digits that repeat forever in a pattern.
  For example 0.121212... or 0.3333...
  Any digits that repeat are written with a dot over them.

  0.$\dot{2}$ represents 0.2222...
  0.$\dot{1}$24$\dot{5}$ represents 0.12451245...

These common fractions are recurring decimals.

$\frac{1}{3} = 0.3333...$ or $0.\dot{3}$ $\frac{2}{3} = 0.6666...$ or $0.\dot{6}$

$\frac{1}{6} = 0.1666...$ or $0.1\dot{6}$ $\frac{1}{11} = 0.090909...$ or $0.\dot{0}\dot{9}$

EXAMPLE

Change these decimals to fractions and give each answer in its simplest form.

a 0.8   b 2.28   c 10.505

a $0.8 = \frac{8}{10} = \frac{4}{5}$

b $2.28 = 2\frac{28}{100} = 2\frac{7}{25}$

c $10.505 = 10\frac{505}{1000} = 10\frac{101}{200}$

EXAMINER'S TIP
Always remember to cancel.

Exercise BN3

MEDIUM

1 Write each of these decimals as a fraction.
   a   0.3
   b   0.03
   c   1.27
   d   11.09
   e   6.101

A calculator must not be used in this exercise.

2 Write each of these decimals as a fraction in its simplest form.
   a   0.4   b   0.05
   c   1.25   d   11.56
   e   6.125   f   12.55
   g   1.405   h   6.508
   i   0.015   j   21.006

3 Which of these decimals are recurring and which are terminating?
   If the decimal is recurring, write out the first 6 digits after the decimal point.
   If the decimal is terminating, write it as a fraction.
   a   0.111
   b   0.$\dot{1}0\dot{1}$
   c   0.502$\dot{7}$
   d   1.2158

4 Elena buys six different scarves and she pays €58.
   She finds the average price by calculating
   €58 ÷ 6 = €9.666 666 666…
   Explain why this is not an exact price.

5 Callum works out 25 ÷ 3 = 8.$\dot{3}$
   He checks this by doing 8.3 × 3
   a   What answer does he get?
   b   Does this mean that Callum got the wrong answer to 25 ÷ 3?
       Explain your answer.

Terminating and recurring decimals

Fractions and decimals

BN4

These headings give the **place value** of a digit in a number.

10 000	1000	100	10	1	.	$\frac{1}{10}$	$\frac{1}{100}$

- The **digit** that is furthest **left** has the biggest value.
  320.3 is bigger than 59.96
  0.1 is bigger than 0.0904

  3 hundreds is bigger than 5 tens (fifty).
  1 tenth is bigger than 9 hundredths.

EXAMPLE

Write these numbers in order, starting with the smallest.
12.2   20   1.99   0.909   43.01

0.909   1.99   12.2   20   43.01

Write the numbers underneath each other with their decimal points in line. The order is obvious.

0.909
1.99
12.2
20
43.01

- You can compare fractions by writing them as **equivalent fractions** with the same denominator.

EXAMPLE

a Which fraction is bigger: $\frac{2}{3}$ or $\frac{3}{4}$?

b Write these fractions in ascending order:
   $\frac{2}{5}$ $\frac{3}{4}$ $\frac{7}{10}$ $\frac{1}{2}$

a $\frac{2}{3} \times \frac{4}{4} = \frac{8}{12}$ and $\frac{3}{4} \times \frac{3}{3} = \frac{9}{12}$

$\frac{9}{12}$ is bigger than $\frac{8}{12}$

so $\frac{3}{4}$ is bigger than $\frac{2}{3}$

Multiply top and bottom of each fraction by the same number so that they each have the same denominator.

b $\frac{2}{5} \times \frac{4}{4} = \frac{8}{20}$ $\frac{3}{4} \times \frac{5}{5} = \frac{15}{20}$ $\frac{7}{10} \times \frac{2}{2} = \frac{14}{20}$ $\frac{1}{2} \times \frac{10}{10} = \frac{10}{20}$

So in ascending order: $\frac{2}{5}$ $\frac{1}{2}$ $\frac{7}{10}$ $\frac{3}{4}$

- You can write a fraction in its **simplest form** by **cancelling**.

EXAMPLE

Cancel each fraction to its simplest form.

a $\frac{18}{24}$

b $3\frac{24}{36}$

a $\frac{18}{24} = \frac{3}{4}$ Divide top and bottom by 6

b $3\frac{24}{36} = 3\frac{2}{3}$ Divide top and bottom by 12

You could divide first by 2 $\left(=\frac{9}{12}\right)$ and then divide by 3.
Always check there are no more common factors.

You could divide in steps by using 2, 3, 4 or 6, but don't leave the answer as $3\frac{12}{18}$ as this is not the simplest form.

Fractions and decimals

Exercise BN4

MEDIUM

1. Copy and complete these equivalent fractions.

   a $\dfrac{3}{4} = \dfrac{}{8} = \dfrac{12}{} = \dfrac{45}{60}$ b $\dfrac{5}{6} = \dfrac{15}{} = \dfrac{}{30} = \dfrac{75}{}$

A calculator must not be used in this exercise.

2. Cancel each fraction to its simplest form.

   a $\dfrac{4}{12}$ b $\dfrac{6}{10}$ c $\dfrac{3}{36}$ d $\dfrac{8}{14}$

   e $\dfrac{9}{18}$ f $\dfrac{7}{28}$ g $\dfrac{16}{36}$ h $\dfrac{240}{360}$

   i $\dfrac{12}{30}$ j $\dfrac{15}{50}$ k $\dfrac{40}{100}$ l $\dfrac{20}{48}$

3. Put each set of numbers in order, starting with the smallest.

   a 102, 97.8, 100.9   b 21.9, 2.19, 219, 0.219
   c 0.3, 0.29, 0.18, 0.1   d 6.07, 6.17, 6.04, 6.18
   e 9, 9.1, 8.9, 9.11   f 3.8, 3.08, 3.79, 3

4. Put each set of fractions in order, starting with the smallest.

   a $\dfrac{3}{4}, \dfrac{1}{2}, \dfrac{1}{4}$ b $\dfrac{2}{3}, \dfrac{5}{12}, \dfrac{5}{6}$ c $\dfrac{3}{10}, \dfrac{4}{5}, \dfrac{13}{20}$

   d $\dfrac{7}{12}, \dfrac{1}{6}, \dfrac{3}{4}$ e $\dfrac{2}{3}, \dfrac{7}{9}, \dfrac{13}{18}$ f $\dfrac{3}{5}, \dfrac{7}{10}, \dfrac{1}{2}, \dfrac{13}{20}$

5. In January Bill spent $\dfrac{3}{5}$ of his income.

   In February he spent $\dfrac{5}{12}$ of his income.

   In which month did Bill spend the larger fraction of his income?

6. Two shipments of glass vases were sent.
   In one shipment, 19 out of the 150 vases were damaged.
   In the second shipment, 7 out of the 50 vases were broken.
   In which shipment was the fraction of broken vases greater?

7. Two breakfast cereals show the following information on the labels.

   Cereal A

Protein	13 g
Carbohydrate	77 g
Fibre	3 g
Other	7 g
Total weight	100 g

   Cereal B

Protein	4 g
Carbohydrate	23 g
Fibre	1 g
Other	2 g
Total weight	30 g

   a Work out the fraction of carbohydrate in each cereal.
   b Which cereal has the greater fraction of fibre?

Fractions and decimals

Calculating with fractions

- To find the decimal equivalent of a fraction, divide the top number by the bottom number.

$$\frac{5}{8} = 5 \div 8 = 0.625 \qquad \frac{1}{3} = 1 \div 3 = 0.3333\ldots \text{ (or 0.33 to 2 dp)}$$

You can use fractions of amounts.

EXAMPLE

a Find $\frac{5}{8}$ of 20 m.   b What fraction is 40 cm of 1 m?

a $20 \div 8 = 2.5$ ($\div$ the amount (20 m) by 8 to find **one** eighth)
   $2.5 \times 5 = 12.5$ m ($\times$ the answer by 5)

b $\frac{40}{100} = \frac{2}{5}$

If the amounts have units, make sure they are the same. Here 100 cm = 1 m

You can add and subtract fractions, but check that the denominators are the same – if they are not, change to equivalent fractions.

EXAMPLE

Calculate:

a $\frac{5}{12} + \frac{11}{12}$ b $\frac{7}{8} - \frac{3}{8}$ c $\frac{5}{6} + \frac{5}{12}$

a $\frac{5}{12} + \frac{11}{12} = \frac{16}{12}$
   $= 1\frac{4}{12} = 1\frac{1}{3}$

b $\frac{7}{8} - \frac{3}{8} = \frac{4}{8} = \frac{1}{2}$

c $\frac{5}{6} + \frac{5}{12} = \frac{10}{12} + \frac{5}{12}$
   $= \frac{15}{12} = 1\frac{3}{12} = 1\frac{1}{4}$

Multiply the top and bottom of $\frac{5}{6}$ by 2, so that the denominators are both 12.

You should also know how to multiply and divide fractions.

EXAMPLE

Calculate:

a $\frac{5}{6} \times 3$ b $\frac{5}{7} \times \frac{2}{3}$ c $\frac{5}{6} \div 3$ d $\frac{5}{7} \div \frac{2}{3}$

a $\frac{5}{6} \times 3 = \frac{5}{6} \times \frac{3}{1} = \frac{15}{6} = 2\frac{1}{2}$

b $\frac{5}{7} \times \frac{2}{3} = \frac{10}{21}$

c $\frac{5}{6} \div 3 = \frac{5}{6} \div \frac{3}{1} = \frac{5}{6} \times \frac{1}{3} = \frac{5}{18}$

d $\frac{5}{7} \div \frac{2}{3} = \frac{5}{7} \times \frac{3}{2} = \frac{15}{14} = 1\frac{1}{14}$

*Write the **integer** as a fraction.*

Multiply both the tops and bottoms.

*If the answer is an **improper fraction**, change to a **mixed number**.*

Turn the second fraction upside down and change the ÷ to a ×.

- The reciprocal of a number is '1 over the number' or 'the fraction turned upside down'.

The reciprocal of $6 = \frac{1}{6}$

The reciprocal of $\frac{2}{3} = \frac{3}{2}$

Exercise BN5

MEDIUM — A calculator must not be used in this exercise.

1 Calculate:
- **a** $\frac{1}{4}$ of £24
- **b** $\frac{3}{4}$ of 30 m
- **c** $\frac{2}{3}$ of 15 km
- **d** $\frac{5}{8}$ of 64 g
- **e** $\frac{3}{5}$ of £12
- **f** $\frac{4}{5}$ of 21 km
- **g** $\frac{2}{3}$ of £11.40
- **h** $\frac{2}{9}$ of 18.09 m

2 Write the first quantity as a fraction of the second.
Give each answer in its simplest possible form.
- **a** 10 cm of 2 m
- **b** 35p of £2
- **c** 1 day of January
- **d** 50 g of 1 kg

3 Calculate:
- **a** $\frac{1}{4} + \frac{1}{4}$
- **b** $\frac{1}{4} \times \frac{1}{4}$
- **c** $\frac{1}{4} \div \frac{1}{4}$
- **d** $\frac{3}{4} - \frac{1}{2}$
- **e** $\frac{3}{8} + \frac{1}{2}$
- **f** $\frac{2}{3} + \frac{1}{5}$
- **g** $\frac{3}{5} \times 6$
- **h** $\frac{2}{7} \div \frac{4}{5}$
- **i** $\frac{5}{8} \times \frac{6}{11}$
- **j** $10 \times \frac{1}{4}$
- **k** $\frac{5}{8} \div \frac{1}{4}$
- **l** $\frac{4}{5} \div 5$

4 Change each of these fractions to a decimal.
If a decimal is recurring, round it correct to 2 dp.
- **a** $\frac{3}{4}$
- **b** $\frac{2}{5}$
- **c** $\frac{3}{8}$
- **d** $\frac{5}{9}$
- **e** $\frac{3}{11}$
- **f** $\frac{3}{20}$

5
- **a** Write down the reciprocal of 8 as a fraction.
- **b** Multiply your answer to part **a** by 8.
- **c** What always happens when you multiply a number by its reciprocal?

6 $\frac{2}{3}$ of the people on a ride were under 15 years old.

$\frac{1}{9}$ of the people were 15 to 19 years old.

What fraction of the people on the ride were over 19 years old?

7 Which of these is the **exact** answer to $\frac{2}{3}$ of £10? Show your working.

A £6.66   **B** £6$\frac{1}{3}$ **C** £6.$\dot{6}$

8 It costs £24 to run a battery–powered car for 7 days.
Here are two statements:

> **A** The average cost to run the car for a day is £3.42.
> **B** The average cost to run the car for a day is £3$\frac{3}{7}$.

Give one reason why **each** statement could be a good answer to the question.

Calculating with fractions

Percentages, fractions and decimals BN6

- A percentage is a fraction with a denominator of 100.
  36% means $\frac{36}{100}$.

$\frac{36}{100}$ cancels to $\frac{9}{25}$.
So $36\% = \frac{9}{25}$

You can also convert between percentages and decimals.
70% = 70 ÷ 100 = 0.7   0.35 = 0.35 × 100% = 35%

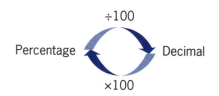

You must learn the relationships shown in this table.
You can work out other facts from them.

Fraction	Decimal	Percentage
$\frac{1}{2}$	0.5	50%
$\frac{1}{4}$	0.25	25%
$\frac{3}{4}$	0.75	15%

Fraction	Decimal	Percentage
$\frac{1}{3}$	0.$\dot{3}$	33.$\dot{3}$%
$\frac{1}{5}$	0.2	20%
$\frac{1}{10}$	0.1	10%

$\frac{2}{3}$ is twice $\frac{1}{3}$, is 33.3% × 2
so $\frac{2}{3}$ = 66.6%

So $\frac{3}{10}$ = 0.3 = 30%

EXAMINER'S TIP
Change a percentage to a decimal by dividing it by 100.

EXAMPLE

a Put these quantities in order of size, starting with the smallest.
0.28, $\frac{1}{4}$, 26%

b Complete this table.

Fraction	Decimal	Percentage
		20%
	0.07	
$\frac{3}{5}$		

a 0.28 × 100 = 28% $\frac{1}{4}$ = 25%
The order is 25%, 26%, 28%
or $\frac{1}{4}$, 26%, 0.28

b

Fraction	Decimal	Percentage
$\frac{1}{5}$	0.2	20%
$\frac{7}{100}$	0.07	7%
$\frac{3}{5}$	0.6	60%

7% means $\frac{7}{100}$ or 7 ÷ 100 = 0.07

Percentages are often used in money contexts.

> **EXAMPLE**
>
> **a** Find 35% of £26.
> **b** Jayne saves £27 when she buys a dress in a sale.
>   Jayne paid £63 for the dress.
>   What percentage was the dress reduced by?
>
> ---
>
> **a** 10% of £26 = 26 ÷ 10 = £2.60
>   30% of £26 = £2.60 × 3 = £7.80
>   5% of £26 = £2.60 ÷ 2 = £1.30
>   So 35% = 30% + 5% = £7.80 + £1.30 = £9.10
>
> **b** $\frac{27}{90} = \frac{3}{10} = \frac{30}{100} = 30\%$
>
> *The dress used to cost 63 + 27 = £90. Cancel by 9 and then $\frac{3}{10} \times \frac{10}{10}$*

Exercise BN6

MEDIUM — A calculator must not be used in this exercise.

1 Write each set of numbers in order, starting with the smallest.

  a 45%, $\frac{1}{2}$, 0.35   **b** 0.07, $\frac{4}{5}$, 70%   **c** $\frac{3}{4}$, 69%, 0.8   **d** 68%, $\frac{2}{3}$, 0.7

2 Which of $\frac{2}{5}$ or 0.52 is the larger? Show how you decide.

3 Celine scores 28 out of 40 in her test. Damien scores 69%.
   Who has the best score? Show how you decide.

4 Xi wants to find 35% of £85. Should he multiply by 3.5, $\frac{3}{5}$, 0.35 or $\frac{35}{10}$?
   Show how you decide.

5 Calculate:
   a 40% of 78 metres   **b** 25% of 88 men   **c** 10% of £5   **d** 60% of £12
   e 15% of 64 g   **f** 1% of 7800   **g** 35% of 80 km **h** 55% of £840
   i 6% of 95 cm   **j** 125% of £44   **k** 45% of 12 metres **l** 21% of 2000

6 John has worked out 19% of £460 as £8.47. Explain whether John is correct or not.

7 Carole buys a savings bond for £2200. She will get 5% interest paid at the end of the year.
   Ian buys his bond for £1500 and gets 7.5% interest paid at the end of the year.
   Who gets the most interest and by how much?

8 $\frac{1}{2}$ is the same as 50%. Show how you can use this fact to write $\frac{7}{8}$ as a percentage.

9 Copy and complete this table.

10 Dan has £480. He wants to earn interest of at least £24 on this money in a year.
    What is the lowest rate of interest he can invest the money at?

Fraction	Decimal	Percentage
	0.01	
		70%
$\frac{2}{5}$		

Percentages, fractions and decimals

Squares and cubes

BN7

The area of a square is $l \times l$ or l^2
(you say: 'l **squared**')

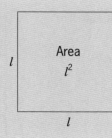

If $l = 6$ cm
Then area $l^2 = 6^2 = 6 \times 6 = 36$ cm²
36 is the **square** of 6.

These are **square numbers** (they are the answers to $1 \times 1, 2 \times 2, 3 \times 3, ..., 15 \times 15$):

1   4   9   16   25   36   49   64
81   100 121 144   169   196   225

You should learn all these numbers.

One side of a square is the
square root of the area.
$l = \sqrt{\text{area}}$

If area $l^2 = 49$ cm²
then one side $l = \sqrt{49} = 7$ cm
7 is the **square root** of 49.

- A square root has two values, one positive and one negative.
  $\sqrt{25} = 5$ and -5 because both $5 \times 5 = 25$ and $-5 \times -5 = 25$
  5 is the positive square root of 25 and -5 is the negative
  square root of 25.

The volume of a cube is $l \times l \times l$ or l^3
(you say: 'l **cubed**')

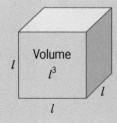

If $l = 4$ cm
Then volume is $l^3 = 4^3 = 64$ cm³
64 is the **cube** of 4.

These are **cube numbers** (they are the answers to $1 \times 1 \times 1, 2 \times 2 \times 2, ..., 10 \times 10 \times 10$):

1   8   27   64   125   216   343   512   729   1000

You should learn all these numbers.

One edge of a cube is the **cube root**
of the volume.
$l = \sqrt[3]{\text{volume}}$

If volume $l^3 = 125$ cm³
then one edge $l = \sqrt[3]{125} = 5$ cm
5 is the **cube root** of 125.

EXAMPLE

a Look at this list of numbers.
   3   8   25   40   64   80

   From the list, write
   i a square number
   ii a number that is both a square number and a cube number.

b Write
   i the cube of 5   ii the negative square root of 100.

a i 25   ii 64
b i 125   ii −10

EXAMINER'S TIP

$\sqrt{100} = 10$.
Just write − in front of 10.

Exercise BN7

MEDIUM

1 Look at this list of numbers.
   1   5   12   17   25   48   91   125   169
   Write
   a A cube number that is also a square number
   b A square number bigger than 30
   c The biggest square number minus the smallest cube number.

   A calculator must not be used in this exercise.

2 Work out the value of
   a The cube of 4
   b The square root of 169
   c 12 squared
   d 20 squared
   e $3^2 + 2^2$
   f $3^2 − 3^2$
   g $5^3 + 2^3$
   h $\sqrt{100}$
   i 14^2
   j 3 cubed − 2 squared

3 Write the whole number that is closest in value to
   a $\sqrt{50}$
   b $\sqrt{80}$
   c $\sqrt{30}$
   d $\sqrt{40}$
   e $\sqrt{120}$
   f $\sqrt{150}$
   g $\sqrt{8}$
   h $\sqrt{5}$

4 The area of a square is 400 cm².
   a How long is one of its sides?
   b What is its perimeter?

5 A wire frame is made in the shape of a cube.
   The frame surrounds 1000 cm³ of air.
   What length of wire is used to make the frame?

Indices and index laws

BN8

You can write repeated multiplications using **indices**, or **powers**.
$12 \times 12 \times 12 = 12^3 \qquad 5 \times 5 \times 5 \times 5 = 5^4$

The base is 12 ⟋ ⟍ The **power** is 3

The index, or power, tells you how many of the base numbers to multiply together.

> 1 index, 2 indices

> If the index is 2, this is called 'squared'.
> $5^2 = 5$ squared
> If the index is 3, this is called 'cubed'.
> $7^3 = 7$ cubed

- When the base number n is the same, you multiply by **adding the indices**.
  $$n^a \times n^b = n^{a+b}$$
  You divide by **subtracting the indices**.
  $$n^a \div n^b = n^{a-b}$$

> These are the **index laws**.

EXAMPLE

a Find the value of each of the following.
  i 5^3 **ii** 2^5 **iii** $5^2 \times 2^3$ **iv** $\dfrac{4^3}{2^5}$

b Simplify each of the following, writing your answer as an index.
  i $4^2 \times 4^3$ **ii** $3^3 \times 3^5$ **iii** $5^3 \times 5 \div 5^2$
  iv $\dfrac{7^2 \times 7^3}{7^4}$ **v** $3^5 \times 2^3 \times 3^3 \times 2$

---

a i $5^3 = 5 \times 5 \times 5$
          $= 25 \times 5$
          $= 125$

ii $2^5 = 2 \times 2 \times 2 \times 2 \times 2$
          $= 4 \quad \times 4 \ \times 2$
          $= 32$

iii $5^2 \times 2^3 = 5 \times 5 \times 2 \times 2 \times 2$
          $= 25 \ \times \ 8$
          $= 200$

iv $\dfrac{4^3}{2^5} = \dfrac{4 \times 4 \times 4}{2 \times 2 \times 2 \times 2 \times 2} = \dfrac{64}{32} = 2$

b i 4^5 **ii** 3^8 **iii** 5^2 **iv** 7 **v** $3^8 \times 2^4$

EXAMINER'S TIP

The rule for multiplying indices only applies when the bases are the same.

A fraction is the same as division. Use the multiplying rule for the numerator $(2 + 3 = 5)$ and then the dividing rule $(5 - 4 = 1)$.
Remember that 7^1 is the same as 7.

Exercise BN8

MEDIUM

A calculator must not be used in this exercise.

1. Write each of these using indices.
   a $2 \times 2 \times 2 \times 2 \times 2 \times 2$
   b $3 \times 3 \times 3$
   c $5 \times 5 \times 5 \times 5 \times 5$
   d $3 \times 2 \times 3 \times 2 \times 3 \times 3$
   e $5 \times 6 \times 6 \times 6 \times 6 \times 5$
   f $10 \times 10 \times 3 \times 3 \times 10$

2. Write each of these as a multiplication of single digits. (Do not do the multiplication.)
   a 4^3
   b 5^4
   c 7^6
   d 8^5
   e $3^3 \times 2^5$
   f $4^3 \times 5^3$
   g $3^2 \times 7^4$
   h $9^3 \times 3^9$

3. Find the value of each of these.
   a 10^3
   b 4^2
   c 1^{12}
   d $2^3 \times 5^2$
   e $4^2 \times 2^2$
   f $12^2 \div 4$
   g $10^2 - 8^2$
   h $\dfrac{6^2}{3^2}$

4. Simplify each of the following, leaving your answer as an index.
   a $2^3 \times 2^4 \times 2^2$
   b $5^3 \times 5^3 \times 5^3$
   c $4^{12} \div 4^3$
   d $3^2 \times 3^4$
   e $6^5 \div 6^3$
   f $5^3 \times 5^2 \div 5^3$
   g $\dfrac{10^3 \times 10^2}{10^4}$
   h $4^3 \times 3^4 \times 4^2 \times 3^2$
   i $7 \times 4^2 \times 7^5 \times 4$
   j $5^3 \times 3^2 \times 5^2 \times 3$
   k $\dfrac{5^3 \times 5 \times 4^3}{4^2 \times 5^2}$
   l $6^2 \times 5^3 \times 6^5 \div 5^2$
   m $3^4 \times 2^5 \div 3^4$
   n $6^4 \div 6^3 \times 4^2 \div 6$
   o $7 \times 7^2 \times 7^3 \div 7^4$

5. Which of 5^3 or 2^8 has the greater value?
   Show your working.

6. 36 is a square number.
   Is 36 also a power of 2?

7. This pattern of numbers continues:
   $2, \ 2^2, \ 2^3, \ 2^4, \ 2^5, \ ...$
   a What is the tenth number in the pattern?
     Write your answer as a power of 2.
   b Write the first six numbers in the sequence as ordinary numbers.
   c What is the answer when you add the **first**
     i two numbers
     ii three numbers
     iii four numbers in the pattern?
   d Show how you can find the total of the first nine numbers in the pattern.
     Do this in **two** different ways.

Indices and index laws

Straight-line graphs

BA1

- Straight-line graphs can be written in the form $y = mx + c$, where m is the **gradient** of the line and c is the **y-intercept**.

← **LOOK BACK**
See topic AA1 to revise letter symbols and the meaning of 'equation', 'formula' and 'expression'.

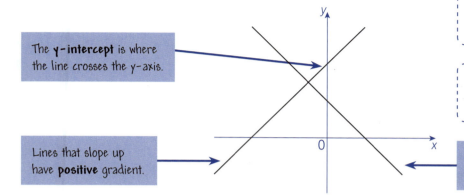

The **y-intercept** is where the line crosses the y-axis.

← **LOOK BACK**
See topic AA2 to revise coordinates.

Lines that slope up have **positive** gradient.

Lines that slope down have **negative** gradient.

- The **gradient** of a line, m, is calculated by finding $\dfrac{\text{vertical change}}{\text{horizontal change}}$.

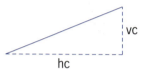

EXAMPLE

Find the gradient of the line $y = 4x + 5$

The gradient is 4.

Look at the number in front of x. It is 4.

- To solve simultaneous equations graphically, draw the straight-line graphs of both equations on the same grid.

EXAMPLE

Use a graphical method to solve $x + y = 6$
$y = x + 1$

First plot the graphs by finding three points on each.

$x + y = 6$

x	0	4	6
y	6	2	0

$y = x + 1$

x	0	2	5
y	1	3	6

Choose any three sensible x-values for each table.
When $x = 5$, $y = 5 + 1 = 6$

Plot the points and join them up with a straight line.

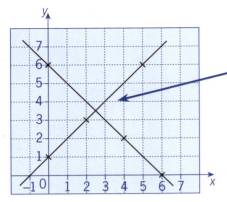

The solution is $x = 2.5$, $y = 3.5$

The graphs cross at the point (2.5, 3.5). This gives you the **solution** of the original equation.

EXAMINER'S TIP

When you are using graphs to solve simultaneous equations, the values may not be whole numbers.

You can check your answer by **substituting** your values into each equation and seeing if both work.

Exercise BA1

MEDIUM HIGH

1 Copy and complete this table of values for the equation $y = x + 3$.

x	−2	2	5
y			8

2 For the following equations, make a table of values and then draw the graphs.
   Draw the graphs for $-4 \leq x \leq 4$.

   a $y = x - 3$ b $y = 2x + 1$ c $y = 3x - 1$

   d $y = 10 - x$ e $x + y = 5$ f $y = \dfrac{x}{2} + 2$

3 Write the gradient and y-intercept of each of these graphs.

   a $y = 6x - 2$ b $y = \dfrac{2}{3}x$ c $y = 8 - x$

4 Find the gradient of the line, L, that passes through (2, 7) and (5, −2).

5 Use the diagram to solve the following pairs of simultaneous equations. Give your answers correct to 1 decimal place.

   a $x + 2y = 10$ b $x + 2y = 10$
      $y = 5x + 3$ $2y - x = 3$

   c $2y - x = 3$
      $y = 5x + 3$

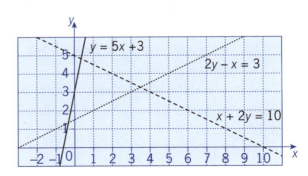

6 Use a graphical method to solve these simultaneous equations. $2x + 3y = 12$
   $y = 2x + 1$

Straight-line graphs

Real-life linear functions BA2

- A **linear function** can be represented with a straight-line graph.
- A linear function of x and y can be written in the form $y = mx + c$.
  This is the **equation** of its straight line.

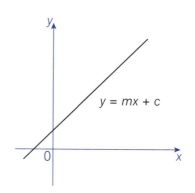

Some real-life situations can be modelled with linear functions.

EXAMPLE

The striped ground cricket makes a fast chirping sound. Scientists measured the number of chirps (N) the striped ground cricket made each second and the temperature (T) in °C.

a Plot these values on a graph, and draw a **line of best fit** through your points.
b How many chirps would you expect to hear per second if the temperature was 30 °C?
c Why would it not be sensible to use your equation to find the number of chirps made at 10 °C?

T	N
31.4	20
22.0	16
34.1	19.8
29.1	18.4
27.0	17.1
24.0	15.5
20.9	14.7
27.8	17.1
20.8	15.4
28.5	16.2
26.4	15
28.1	17.2
27.0	16
28.6	17
24.6	14.4

a [Graph showing N plotted against T with line of best fit]

To draw a line of best fit, move your ruler until approximately half the points are above the line and half below.

b Reading the value of N when $T = 30$ from the line of best fit, you would expect to hear about 17.5–18 chirps per second.

c 10 °C is outside of the range that you have data for. Therefore you do not know if the rule will still be valid.

EXAMINER'S TIP

As this question uses 'real' data the points do not lie exactly on a straight line, so you need to draw a line of best fit. In some situations the points may lie exactly on a straight line.

Exercise BA2

MEDIUM

1 For each of the following data sets:
   i plot the points
   ii draw a line through the points (it may either be exact or a line of best fit)
   Draw each graph on a separate set of axes and choose scales
   to make each graph as large as possible.

a		b		c		d		e		f	
m	r	g	n	t	R	w	s	n	Q	r	b
3	37	3	13	3	24	3	0	23	18	132	8
10	72	10	24	10	22	10	38	32	22	286	32
8	62	8	21	8	23	8	33	19	16	417	60
21	127	21	42	21	19	21	100	22	18	333	47
32	182	32	60	32	15	32	185	30	22	613	110
12	82	12	28	12	21	12	46	16	14	541	83
43	237	43	77	43	12	43	230	29	21	189	19
26	152	26	50	26	17	26	138	26	17	377	54

2 Barney is cooking roast beef for his family. He looks in a recipe book for cooking instructions and then looks on the Internet.

The recipe book leads to a formula of $C = 20w + 20$ where C is the cooking time in minutes and w is the weight of the beef in pounds.

a Write a formula for the cooking time based on the Internet recipe.
b On the same set of axes, draw graphs to represent the cooking times for **both** sets of instructions for $0 \leq w \leq 6$.
c Use your graphs to find the weight of beef for which **both** sets of instructions give the **same** cooking time.
d Form and solve an equation in w to verify your answer from part **c**.

3 Juliet thinks there is a linear relationship between the length of a plane flight and the cost of a ticket. She looked up the price of the cheapest one-way ticket on 1st September with the same national airline from London to each of these destinations. She found their distance from London using the Internet.

City	Paris	Berlin	Prague	Helsinki	Brussels	Warsaw	Lyon	Oslo
Distance (m)	213	578	643	1131	198	899	458	716
Cost (£)	59	73	105	74	69	79	69	68

a Plot this data on a grid and draw a line of best fit through the points.
b Comment on Juliet's idea.

Real-life linear functions

Inequalities

BA3

- An **inequality** is a mathematical statement involving one or more of these **symbols**:
  - $<$ means 'less than'
  - $\leq$ means 'less than or equal to'
  - $>$ means 'greater than'
  - $\geq$ means 'greater than or equal to'

$x > 3$ means that x can take any value greater than 3 (for example, 3.01, 4, $4\frac{3}{7}$, 5, 6, 7, ...)

$x \leq 1$ means that x can take any value less than or equal to 1 (for example, 1, $\frac{1}{3}$, 0, –1, –2, –3.903, ...)

- Inequalities can be represented on a **number line**.

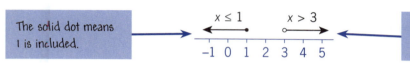

The solid dot means 1 is included.

The empty dot means 3 is **not** included.

A statement can contain two inequalities.
$-2 \leq x < 3$ means that x can take any value between –2 and 3, but not including 3.

- Inequalities are solved using **inverse operations** in the same way as linear equations.
  - The one exception is that if you **multiply** or **divide** each side by a **negative number** you **reverse** the inequality.

  Consider the inequality $\quad 6 > 4$
  Multiply by –2: $\quad 6 \times -2 < 4 \times -2$
  Divide by –2: $\quad 6 \div -2 < 4 \div -2$

EXAMPLE

Solve these inequalities.
Represent the answer to part **c** on a number line.

a $3x - 7 \leq 23$ **b** $4 - 2x > 10$ **c** $11 \leq 5m + 6 < 26$

If you started by adding 2x to each side, you could avoid dividing by a negative.

a $3x - 7 \leq 23$
   $3x \leq 30$ Add 7 to each side
   $x \leq 10$ Divide each side by 3

b $4 - 2x > 10$
   $-2x > 6$ Subtract 4 from each side
   $x < -3$ Divide by –2 so reverse inequality

c $11 \leq 5m + 6 < 26$
   $5 \leq 5m < 20$ Subtract 6 from each term
   $1 \leq m < 4$ Divide each term by 5

Exercise BA3

MEDIUM

1 Represent each of these inequalities on a separate number line.
  a $x \geq 3$
  b $x > 4$
  c $x < 1$
  d $x \leq 0$
  e $x > -4$
  f $x \leq -2$
  g $2 < x \leq 6$
  h $-3 \leq x < 1$
  i $-2\frac{3}{4} < x < -1\frac{1}{2}$

2 Solve each of these inequalities.
  a $x + 3 > 9$
  b $8x > 40$
  c $x - 9 < 16$
  d $\frac{y}{6} \leq 10$
  e $2x + 3 \geq 10$
  f $4p - 7 \leq 11$
  g $\frac{d}{3} - 4 > 2$
  h $\frac{f}{5} + 6 < 9$
  i $3(r - 2) > 1$
  j $2(3x + 5) \geq 2 - 2x$
  k $3 - 5x > -2$
  l $-3x \leq 30$
  m $2 - v \leq 5 - 7v$
  n $5c + 6 > 3c + 2(6 - c)$
  o $\frac{r}{3} > \frac{r+2}{2}$
  p $-1 < 2x < 10$
  q $3 < x + 5 < 12$
  r $5 \leq 2x - 9 \leq 14$

3 Represent your answers to question **2** parts **a**, **e**, **i**, **m** and **q** on number lines.

4 Dave has 3 packets of mints and 7 loose mints.
Ann has 1 packet of mints and 25 loose mints.
Dave has **at least** as many mints as Ann.

Let m be the number of mints in a packet.
Form and solve an inequality in m.
What is the **smallest** number of mints that could be in each packet?

Inequalities

Basic geometry

BG1

Learn these angle facts.

Angles at a point add up to 360°.

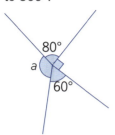

$a + 80° + 90° + 60° = 360°$
$a = 360° - 230° = 130°$

Opposite angles are equal.

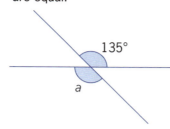

$a = 135°$

Angles that make up a half turn add up to 180°.

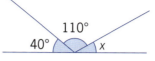

$x + 40° + 110° = 180°$
$x = 180° - 150° = 30°$

You should learn the rules for angles and parallel lines.

Alternate angles are equal.

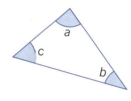

$x = y$

Corresponding angles are equal.

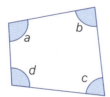

$a = b$

Interior angles sum to 180°.

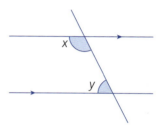

$x + y = 180°$

Remember these facts about angles in a triangle or a quadrilateral.

Triangle

$a + b + c = 180°$

Quadrilateral

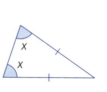

$a + b + c + d = 360°$

Remember these triangles:

Isosceles

Equilateral

EXAMPLE

Find the unknown angles shown by letters in these diagrams (which are not drawn to scale).

a

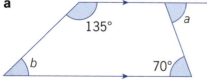

b

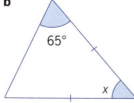

c

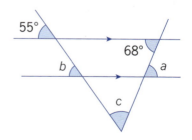

a $a = 70°$ (alternate)
$b = 180° - 135° = 45°$
(interior angles)

b $x = 180° - 2 \times 65°$
$= 50°$

c $a = 68°$ (alternate)
$b = 55°$ (corresponding)
$c = 180° - (68° + 55°) = 57°$
(triangle sum)

> **EXAMPLE**
>
> Find the unknown angles, giving reasons for your answers.
>
>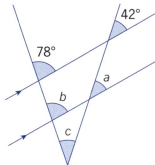
>
> a = 85° (alternate)
> b = 70° (alternate)
> c = 180° − (70° + 85°) = 25° (triangle sum)
> d = 25° (opposite angles equal)

Exercise BG1

MEDIUM

1 Find the unknown angles.

a

b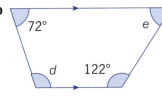

c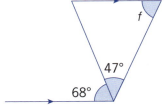

2 Find the unknown angles, giving reasons for your answers.

a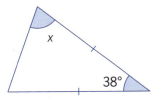

b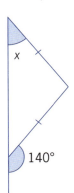

c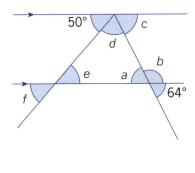

3 Using this diagram and the properties of parallel lines, explain carefully why the sum of the three angles in any triangle must be 180°.

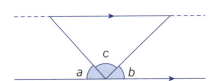

Basic geometry

Polygons and quadrilaterals

A **quadrilateral** is a polygon with four sides. There are several different types of quadrilateral and they each have their own properties.

← **LOOK BACK**
See topic AG1 to revise scales and units.

square

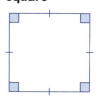

rhombus

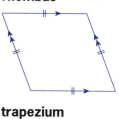

rectangle

parallelogram

trapezium

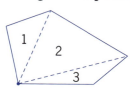

kite

A five-sided **polygon** is called a **pentagon** and a six-sided polygon is a **hexagon**. You can use the fact that the interior angles of a triangle sum to 180° to work out the sum of the interior angles of a pentagon and a hexagon.

A polygon is a closed shape with straight edges.

You can divide a pentagon into 3 triangles so the sum of its 5 interior angles must be $3 \times 180° = 540°$

You can divide a hexagon into 4 triangles so the sum of its 6 interior angles = $4 \times 180° = 720°$

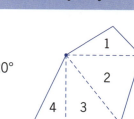

The sum of the exterior angles of any polygon is always 360°. These are the exterior angles of

a quadrilateral

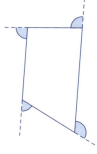

a pentagon

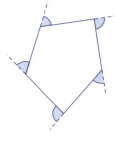

*Polygons with all sides equal and all angles equal are called **regular** polygons.*

EXAMPLE

Find the unknown angles in this pentagon.

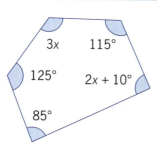

The sum of the interior angles of a pentagon
= $3 \times 180° = 540°$
$5x + 335° = 540°$
$\quad\quad 5x = 205°$
$\quad\quad\quad x = 205° \div 5$
$\quad\quad\quad\quad = 41°$

The unknown angles are $3 \times 41° = 123°$
and $2 \times 41° + 10° = 92°$

76 Polygons and quadrilaterals

EXAMPLE

Find the size of one exterior angle of a regular pentagon.
Hence find the interior angle.

Exterior angle = $\frac{360°}{5}$ = 72°

Interior angle = 180° − 72° = 108°

Exercise BG2

MEDIUM

1 Find the unknown angles in these diagrams.

a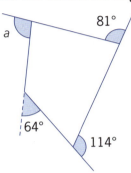
b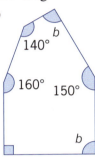
c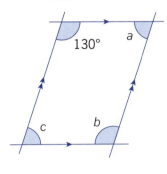

2 a By dividing the octagon into triangles, find the total interior angle sum for an octagon.

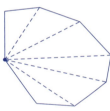

b Use this fact to calculate the size of angle x in this diagram.

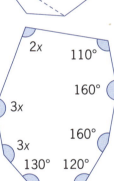

3 a David wants to draw a regular pentagon. He starts by drawing a circle radius 4 cm.
Write down clear instructions so that he can draw a regular pentagon using this circle.
b How could he draw a regular hexagon?
c Write instructions that work for any polygon.

4 A garden is designed in the shape of a regular enneagon (9-sided polygon). Calculate the size of one interior angle of this polygon and hence the size of one exterior angle.

This is also called a nonagon.

5 a Find the total interior angle sum for a regular 20-sided polygon. Hence find the size of one interior angle.
b Show that this is correct by calculating the size of one exterior angle of the polygon and using this to find the size of an interior angle. In both cases, explain carefully what your method is.

6 Could regular pentagons be used to tile a floor leaving no spaces? What about regular hexagons? Explain your answers clearly.

Tiling without leaving spaces is called tessellation.

Polygons and quadrilaterals

Translations

BG3

When you **translate** an **object** you change its position without rotating, reflecting or enlarging it.

You describe a translation with a **column vector** $\begin{pmatrix} x \\ y \end{pmatrix}$.

> x is the number of units moved left or right, y is the number of units moved up or down.

For example

$\begin{pmatrix} 4 \\ -1 \end{pmatrix}$ means you move the object 4 units right and 1 unit down.

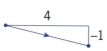

The vector $\begin{pmatrix} -4 \\ -2 \end{pmatrix}$ describes a translation from $(1, 5)$ to $(-3, 3)$.

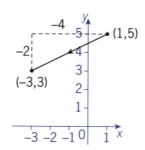

> The point $(-3, 3)$ is the **image** of the point $(1, 5)$ under the translation $\begin{pmatrix} -4 \\ -2 \end{pmatrix}$.

EXAMPLE

Write the vector which translates $(1, 3)$ to

a $(5, 4)$ b $(-4, 6)$ c $(-3, -2)$

a $\begin{pmatrix} 4 \\ 1 \end{pmatrix}$ b $\begin{pmatrix} -5 \\ 3 \end{pmatrix}$ c $\begin{pmatrix} -4 \\ -5 \end{pmatrix}$

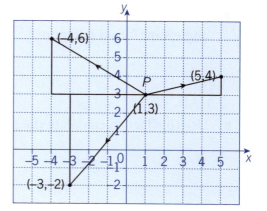

EXAMPLE

a Translate triangle ABC using the vector $\begin{pmatrix} 2 \\ 3 \end{pmatrix}$ and label the **image** $A'B'C'$.

b Which vector would translate $A'B'C'$ to ABC?

a

b The vector that translates triangle $A'B'C'$ to triangle ABC is $\begin{pmatrix} -2 \\ -3 \end{pmatrix}$

> Changing the sign of a vector changes its direction.
> $-\begin{pmatrix} 2 \\ 3 \end{pmatrix} = \begin{pmatrix} -2 \\ -3 \end{pmatrix}$

Exercise BG3

MEDIUM

1. Find the image of the point (1, 4) when translated by the following vectors.

   a $\begin{pmatrix} 6 \\ 2 \end{pmatrix}$ b $\begin{pmatrix} 5 \\ -3 \end{pmatrix}$ c $\begin{pmatrix} 0 \\ -4 \end{pmatrix}$ d $\begin{pmatrix} 3 \\ 0 \end{pmatrix}$ e $\begin{pmatrix} -1 \\ -6 \end{pmatrix}$

2. On a coordinate grid, plot the triangle with vertices $A(1, -1)$, $B(3, 0)$ and $C(2, 1)$.
   Translate triangle ABC using the vector $\begin{pmatrix} -1 \\ 3 \end{pmatrix}$.

   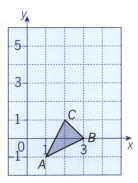

   Which vector would translate the image triangle back to the original triangle?

3. Tom is playing a game following instructions given by Moira. Moira holds up a card showing Tom a vector which tells him how many paces he must make towards or away from her and how many paces north or south of where she is standing.

   For example, if Moira shows Tom $\begin{pmatrix} 4 \\ -3 \end{pmatrix}$ then he will walk 4 paces towards her and then 3 paces south of her.

   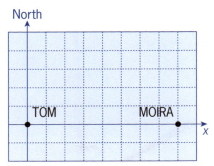

   If Moira holds up these instructions

   $\begin{pmatrix} 3 \\ 2 \end{pmatrix}$, $\begin{pmatrix} 2 \\ 1 \end{pmatrix}$, $\begin{pmatrix} -1 \\ -5 \end{pmatrix}$, $\begin{pmatrix} 0 \\ 3 \end{pmatrix}$

   a show Tom's movements on a copy of the grid
   b work out the final vector that will move Tom to where Moira is standing.

Translations

Symmetry, reflection and rotation

An equilateral triangle has three lines of **reflection** symmetry (sometimes called line symmetry) and **rotation** symmetry of order 3.

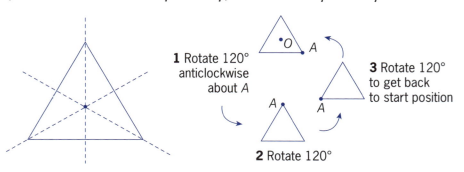

Every shape has rotation symmetry of at least order 1 (a complete turn brings the shape back to its original position).

☒ A line of symmetry divides a shape into identical halves.

EXAMPLE

Write down the number of lines of symmetry and the order of rotation symmetry of these shapes.

a   rectangle

b   octagon

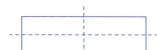

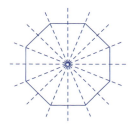

a   2 lines of symmetry
    rotation symmetry order 2

b   16 lines of symmetry
    rotation symmetry order 8

A parallelogram has no lines of reflection symmetry. You can **justify** this by looking at point X.

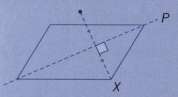

The image of X is not on the parallelogram. Now look at the other diagonal.

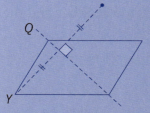

The image of Y is not on the parallelogram either.

- You describe a rotation by naming the **centre** and the **angle** of rotation. Anticlockwise rotations are positive and clockwise rotations are negative.
- You describe a reflection by naming the **mirror line**.

EXAMPLE

a   Reflect the triangle A in the line $x = 3$.
b   Rotate the triangle A through 90° about the centre (2, 0).
c   Reflect the triangle A in the line $y = 0$.

Points on the mirror line don't move.

The line $y = 0$ is the x-axis.

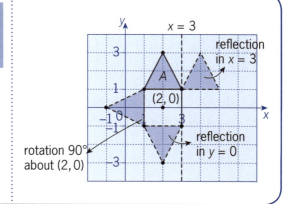

Exercise BG4

MEDIUM

1. Copy the diagram and use the lines of symmetry to draw the complete shapes.
   What is the order of rotation symmetry of each shape?

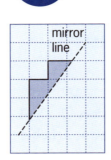
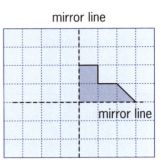

2. Reflect triangle K in
   a. the x-axis
   b. the line y = 1
   c. the line y = x

3. On axes labelled from −6 to 6, plot A(1, 1), B(4, 2), C(3, 4) and join the points to make triangle ABC.
   a. Rotate triangle ABC clockwise through 90° about (−1, 0) and label the image triangle T.
   b. Reflect T in the y-axis and label the image U.

4. Copy and complete this table.

Regular polygon	Number of mirror lines	Order of rotation symmetry
Equilateral triangle		
Square		
Pentagon		
Hexagon		
Heptagon		
Octagon		

What do you notice?

5. Describe fully the transformation of trapezium A onto
   a. T_1
   b. T_2

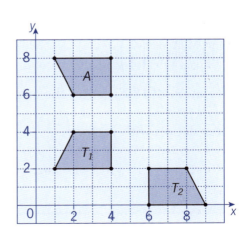

6. What single reflection is equivalent to a reflection in the line x = 1, followed by a reflection in the line x = 3, followed by a reflection in the line x = 6?

Symmetry, reflection and rotation

Combining transformations

BG5

You can map an object onto its final image using two (or more) transformations.

EXAMPLE

The triangle P has vertices (2, 1), (4, 1) and (4, 2).
a Reflect P in the line $x = 2$. Label the image A.
   Reflect triangle A in the line $x = 3$ and label the image B.
   What single transformation would map P directly onto B?
b Reflect triangle P in the y-axis. Label the image triangle Q.
   Reflect Q in the x-axis and label the image R.
   What single transformation would map triangle R back onto the original triangle P?

a The single transformation equivalent to these two reflections would be a translation with the vector $\begin{pmatrix} 2 \\ 0 \end{pmatrix}$.

b Either by observation or using tracing paper you can see that a rotation of 180°, centre the origin, would map R back onto P.

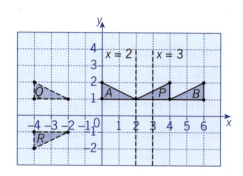

EXAMPLE

Using the diagram below describe fully the transformation of
a A onto F and then F onto E
b A onto G and then G onto H

a Rotation of 90°, centre (0, −1), followed by a translation with vector $\begin{pmatrix} 0 \\ 2 \end{pmatrix}$.

b Rotation of 180°, centre the origin, followed by a translation with vector $\begin{pmatrix} -2 \\ 0 \end{pmatrix}$.

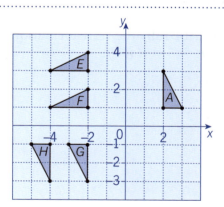

Exercise BG5

MEDIUM

1 *P* is the point with coordinates (3, 3).

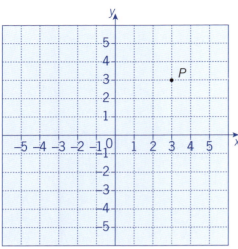

a *P* is reflected in the *x*-axis and then translated by the vector $\begin{pmatrix} -5 \\ 0 \end{pmatrix}$. Find the coordinates of the final image of *P*.

b i *P* is rotated through 90°, centre (2, 1) and then reflected in the line *x* = −1. Write the coordinates of the final image of *P*.
   ii What single translation would map *P* directly onto the final image?

2 Using the diagram below, describe the following transformations.
   a *C* to *I* and *I* to *E*
   b *B* to *A* and *A* to *H*

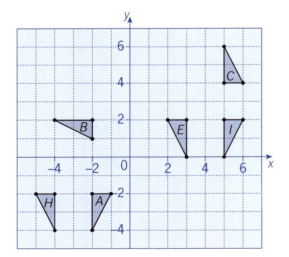

3 A triangle *P* has vertices (0, 3), (1, 0) and (0, −1).
   a What single transformation of *P* is equivalent to a reflection in the line *x* = 1 followed by a reflection in the line *x* = 4?
   b What single transformation of *P* is equivalent to a reflection in the line *y* = 2 followed by a reflection in the line *y* = −1?
   c Try some double reflections of your own. What conclusions can you make? Express your conclusions clearly.

Congruence and similarity BG6

- Shapes which are identical in every respect are said to be **congruent**.

One shape could be picked up and placed exactly on top of the other.
Triangle A in the diagram could be flipped over and then placed exactly on top of the other triangle B.

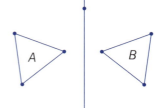

- Mathematically **similar** shapes are identical in their shape but are enlargements or reductions of each other. Similar shapes have corresponding angles equal and corresponding sides in the same proportion.

Shape B is the same as shape A, but its sides are double the length.

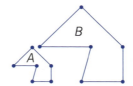

To decide if two triangles are similar it is sufficient to show the angles are the same in both triangles. This can often be checked using the angle sum property for triangles (ie angles sum to 180°).

EXAMPLE

Show that the following pairs of triangles are similar.

a
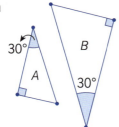

b
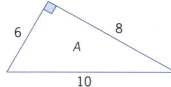
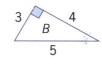

a Using the angle sum property for triangles the missing angle for A is 30° and for B is 60° hence both triangles have the same angles and are therefore similar.

b Clearly triangle B is half the size of A and therefore the triangles are similar.

Exercise BG6

MEDIUM

1. Are the following pairs of triangles similar? Give reasons for your answers.

   a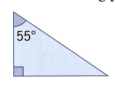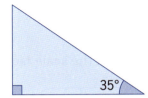

   b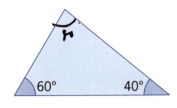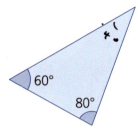

   c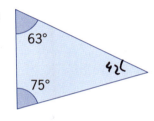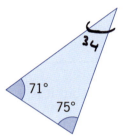

   d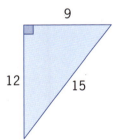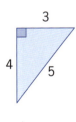

2. Match the congruent triangles.

   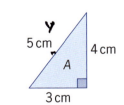 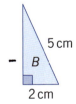

   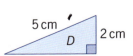 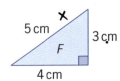

Congruence and similarity

Enlargements

BG7

- **Congruent** shapes are identical.
- If two shapes are **similar** one is an enlargement of the other. They have the same angles but may be different sizes.

You describe an **enlargement** by naming the **centre** and the **scale factor**.

EXAMPLE

Enlarge triangle P with centre O and scale factor 2.

 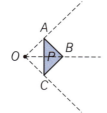 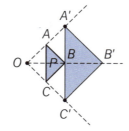

Draw rays through A, B and C from O.

$OA' = 2OA$
$OB' = 2OB$
$OC' = 2OC$

When you enlarge an object the image can be smaller but it is still called an enlargement.

EXAMPLE

Plot the points $A(3, 2)$, $B(6, 2)$, $C(5, 4)$ and $D(4, 4)$ and join them up to form a trapezium.

a Using the point $(5, 1)$ as the centre of enlargement, enlarge the trapezium with scale factor 2.

b Using centre $(4, 6)$ enlarge the trapezium with scale factor $\frac{1}{2}$.

a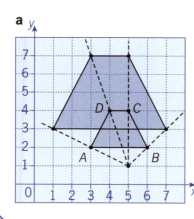

b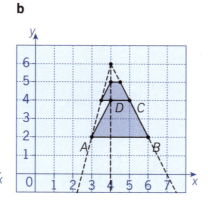

86 Enlargements

Exercise BG7

MEDIUM

1 Copy the diagram. Use the centre of enlargement to enlarge the shape with scale factor 3.

> Do a rough sketch first to make sure you have enough space.

2 Copy the diagram on to a grid and, on three separate diagrams, enlarge the shape ABCDE with
   a scale factor 2, centre (0, 0)
   b scale factor 0.5, centre (6, 6)
   c scale factor 0.75, centre (2, 3)

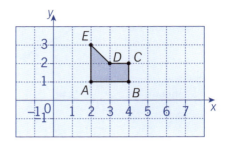

3 **a** Join the points $A(5, 3)$, $B(9, 7)$, $C(13, -1)$ and $D(7, -1)$ to form a quadrilateral.
   b Using (5, 1) as the centre of enlargement, enlarge ABCD with scale factor $\frac{1}{2}$.
   c Write the coordinates of the vertices of the image quadrilateral.

4 Fraser has a photograph measuring 15 cm × 10 cm. Could this photograph be mathematically enlarged to the following dimensions? Provide clear reasoning for your answers.
   a 30 cm × 20 cm   **b** 18.75 cm × 12.5 cm   **c** 7.5 cm × 6 cm
   d 3 cm × 2 cm   **e** 67.5 cm × 45 cm   **f** 52.5 cm × 33.5 cm

5 Trapezium P is drawn on a grid as shown.

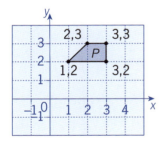

   a Copy the grid. Draw the enlarged image of P with scale factor 2 and centre of enlargement (0, 0). Label the image Q.
   b Now draw the enlarged image of P with scale factor 2 and centre of enlargement (4, 4). Label this image R.
   c Describe the transformation from Q to R.

Enlargements   87

The language of circles

BG8

You need to know the names of the different parts of a circle.

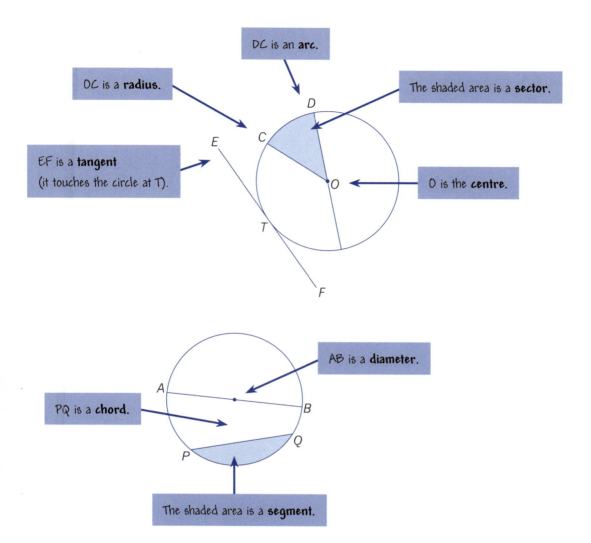

OC is a **radius**.
DC is an **arc**.
The shaded area is a **sector**.
EF is a **tangent** (it touches the circle at T).
O is the **centre**.
AB is a **diameter**.
PQ is a **chord**.
The shaded area is a **segment**.

EXAMPLE

Draw a circle so that the line AB is the radius.

A ——— B

Put the point of the **compasses** at A or B and open the compasses to the length of AB.
Draw the circle.

Exercise BG8

MEDIUM

1 Link each letter on the diagram with the appropriate word in the list.

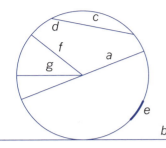

tangent   chord
sector   radius
arc   diameter
segment

2 Measure
   a the diameter of the circle
   b the radius of the circle.

3 a Draw a circle with a radius of 4 cm.
   b Draw a chord of length 5 cm inside the circle.

4 Draw a circle with a diameter of 10 cm.

5 a Draw a 4 cm line *AB*.
   b Draw a circle so that *AB* is the diameter.
   c Find the radius of the circle.

6 Use a protractor and compasses to construct these sectors.

a 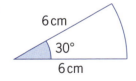   b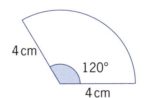

7 Two circles have the same centre.
   One has a radius of 3.5 cm and the other has a radius of 2.5 cm.
   Construct and colour this diagram for the two circles.

8 Explain why these circles are similar.

 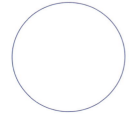

The language of circles 89

Scatter graphs BS1

- A **scatter graph** shows how two sets of numerical data are related.
- **Correlation** is a measure of how the data are related.

You should discuss **correlation** in terms of the direction of the scattered points (positive or negative) and by how much the points appear to lie on a straight line (strong or weak). When there is good correlation between matched pairs of data you can draw a **line of best fit**.

> A **line of best fit** is a straight line with points evenly distributed either side. It does not have to pass through the origin.

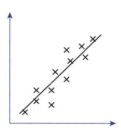

Positive correlation forms a line with positive gradient.

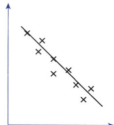

Negative correlation forms a line with negative gradient.

Zero correlation occurs when it is not possible to draw a line of best fit.

EXAMPLE

The diagram shows the correlation between engine capacity, in cm^3, and fuel consumption on motorway journeys, in miles per gallon (mpg), for 8 cars.

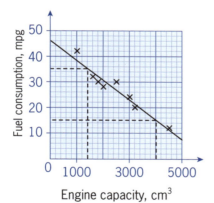

a Explain why it is appropriate to draw a line of best fit.
b Describe the correlation.
c Use the line of best fit to estimate
   i fuel consumption for 4000 cm^3 engine capacity
   ii engine capacity for a car with fuel consumption 35 mpg.

a The points look like they lie on a straight line.
b Strong negative correlation; as engine capacity increases, fuel consumption decreases.
c i 15 mpg   ii 1400 cm^3

Scatter graphs

Exercise BS1

1 Look at the scatter diagrams below and fully describe any correlation shown.
   You may want to use words such as:
   Strong   Weak   Moderate   No correlation   Positive   Negative

2 The table shows the scores of a multiplication test and a division test taken by a group of ten students.

Multiplication	25	18	15	20	16	12	14	20	18	9
Division	22	19	17	21	14	14	15	19	16	12

a Draw a scatter graph to display these data.
b Describe any correlation shown by your graph.
c Draw a line of best fit.
d Another student had taken the multiplication test and scored 23.
   Use your graph to predict her score on the division test.
e Explain why it may be difficult to use this graph to predict the score in the division test for a student who scored 6 on the multiplication test.

3 The transition times, T1 and T2 in seconds, for 12 of the first 13 competitors to finish the 2009 London triathlon male sprint distance are recorded in the table.

T1	163	153	160	171	214	164	260	176	198	144	169	198
T2	113	114	108	106	148	132	106	106	161	109	111	138

a Draw a scatter diagram for these data.
b T1 is the time taken to change sport from swim to bike and T2 the time taken to change sport from bike to run.
   Comment on the T1 and T2 times shown by your scatter diagram.
c Part of the data for one of the first 13 males to finish this triathlon is missing.
   His T1 time was 209 seconds. If it is possible, use your graph to estimate his T2 time, if it is not possible explain why it is not possible.

4 The table shows the weights, to the nearest kg, and the bleep test scores for a sample of students.

Weight, kg	45	60	57	62	48	54	49	44
Bleep test score	7.8	6.0	6.3	5.8	7.1	6.5	7.3	7.5

a Draw a scatter diagram to show these data.
b Describe any correlation shown by your graph.
c Draw a line of best fit on your graph.
d Use your line to estimate   i   the weight of a student with a bleep test score of 6.8
                                ii the bleep test score of a student who weighs 51 kg.

Time series　　BS2

A **time series** graph displays several values of a measurement taken at different times.

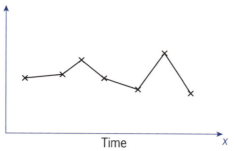

Time is always on the horizontal axis.

- The **trend** of a time series graph shows the general direction of the measurements over a period of time.
- **Seasonal variations** are where the patterns match to seasons of the year, for example heating costs (more in winter than summer).
- **Cyclical variations** are where the general shape of the graph has a tendency to repeat.
- **Random variations** are unpredictable and can appear in any time series graph.

EXAMPLE

The graph shows the percentage of trains operated by one company that arrived late during 2009.

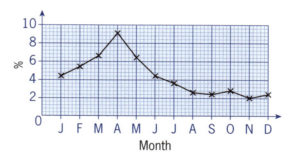

a Describe the trend shown by the graph.
b These are the percentages of late trains for the first eight months of the following year.

Month	Jan	Feb	March	April	May	June	July	Aug
% late	2.2	3	2.8	3.4	2.5	2.1	1.8	2

Describe any further trends in the data.
c Comment, with reasons, on whether the train company improved its punctuality.

a Increase in number of late trains in first few months, but towards the end of the year only approximately 2% of trains were late.
b It appears that the trend follows the same pattern as the previous year with an increase to a peak in April and then a decrease.
c The trend appears to be the same in both years. In the second year, the peak in April is lower, also the months leading up to that have a

Give mathematical reasons.
As well as a reason give a final conclusion to answer the question.

Exercise BS2

1. The number of ASBOs, to the nearest 100, issued each year from 2002 to 2008 are given in the table.

Year	2002	2003	2004	2005	2006	2007	2008
ASBOs	400	1300	3500	4100	2700	2300	2000

   a Draw a time series graph to represent these data.
   b Comment on any trend shown by your graph.

2. The graph shows the temperature, taken at 4-hourly intervals, of a hospital patient suffering from a virus.

   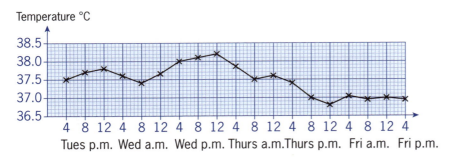

   a When was the patient most ill?
   b Normal temperature is 36.9 °C. When would you say the patient's temperature begins to return to normal? Give mathematical reasons for your answer.

3. The table gives the termly sales turnover, to the nearest £100, for a school canteen.

	2004	2005	2006	2007
Spring		£4500	£4700	£5000
Summer		£3800	£4000	£4100
Autumn	£5600	£6200	£6500	

   a Plot the data on a time series graph.
   b Describe the trend shown by the graph.

4. A beach café is open all year round. The table shows its quarterly sales figures, to the nearest £100, for 3 years.

	Jan–Mar	Apr–June	July–Sept	Oct–Dec
2007	£4000	£6200	£10 000	£5300
2008	£4200	£6500	£12 400	£4700
2009	£4000	£6600	£15 000	£5400

   a Plot the data on a time series graph.
   b Describe the trend shown by the graph.
   c One winter was particularly cold. Which winter do you think that was and why?

Calculating with fractions and rounding CN1

You should know how to calculate a fraction of an amount.

EXAMPLE

a Akhtar and Ruby raise £360 for charity.
   Akhtar raises $\frac{7}{12}$ of the money. How much does Ruby raise?

b Karen has 350 fliers to deliver. After 2 hours she has delivered 105 of them.
   What fraction of the fliers has she delivered?

a $\frac{5}{12} \times \frac{360}{1} = \frac{5 \times 360}{12} = £150$

b $\frac{105}{350} = \frac{21}{70} = \frac{3}{10}$

You can enter fractions on your calculator. Some calculators have this key:

You can use either a written or a calculator method to add, subtract, multiply or divide fractions.

EXAMPLE

a Brian, Jenny and Sean share the cost of a meal.
   Brian eats most and pays $\frac{9}{20}$ of the bill, and Jenny pays $\frac{2}{5}$ of the bill.
   What fraction of the bill does Sean pay?

b Show that $25 \div 10$ is the same as $\frac{1}{10}$ of 25.

Sheraton Restaurant
Emwell street, Warminster.

1 Chilli con carne & rice	xxxx
1 Roast chicken with potatoes	xxxx
1 Mushroom pizza	xxxx
1 Jelly yoghurt fruit salad	xxxx
Total charge	xxxx

Thank You!

a $\frac{9}{20} + \frac{2}{5} = \frac{9}{20} + \frac{8}{20} = \frac{17}{20}$

Sean pays $1 - \frac{17}{20} = \frac{3}{20}$

b $25 \div 10 = 2.5$ $\frac{1}{10} \times 25 = \frac{25}{10} = 2.5$
   They are the same.

Multiply $\frac{2}{5}$ by $\frac{4}{4}$ to get a common denominator.
OR
Enter the fractions on your calculator and add.

"of" is the same as × using fractions.

You should know how to round to a number of significant figures.
Start at the left of the number. The first significant figure is the first digit that is **not 0**.
2.3158 to 3sf = 2.32
0.003 516 to 2sf = 0.0035

sf is an abbreviation for significant figures.

Do not round answers to stages in working.
Only round the final answer.

← **LOOK BACK**
See Topic AN3 to further revise rounding.

EXAMPLE

a A merchant pays £25.37 for 9 identical bags of grain. How much would he pay for 16 bags?
b A lift can carry a maximum of 5 people. 36 people want to go to floor 27.
   How many trips will the lift make?

a 1 bag costs £25.37 ÷ 9 = £2.81888…
   16 bags cost £2.81888… × 16 = £45.10222 or £45.10

b 36 ÷ 5 = 7.2
   The lift will make 8 trips.

It would be wrong to round 7.2 down. Always look at the context of the problem.

Exercise CN1

 MEDIUM

1. In a Lucky Dip, tickets are only red, green or yellow.
   Of the tickets, $\frac{2}{5}$ are red and $\frac{1}{3}$ are green.
   What fraction of the tickets is yellow?

2. Round each of these numbers to the required number of significant figures.
   a 3.406 84   to 1sf
   b 3.406 84   to 3sf
   c 13.417   to 2sf
   d 17 406.1   to 3sf
   e 0.004 39   to 2sf
   f 0.000 0039 986   to 2sf

3. Electricity is sold for a cost of 14.824p per unit of electricity.
   Shona uses an average of 5.8 units each day for a week.
   How much does Shona pay for the week's electricity?

4. Tina manages a hotel that has 54 rooms.
   One day 36 of the rooms have people staying in them.
   What fraction of the rooms in the hotel is **empty**?

5. Show that 3.6 is $\frac{1}{9}$ of 32.4 using a multiplication.

6. Habib has to paint one side of a wall that is 4 m high and 25 m long.
   He can paint 30 m² of the wall in a day.
   a How many days will it take him to paint the wall?
   b After $2\frac{1}{2}$ days, how many square metres of the wall does he still have to paint?
   c What fraction of the wall has he painted after 2 days?

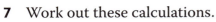

7. Work out these calculations.
   a $\frac{2}{3} - \frac{2}{5}$
   b $\frac{1}{6} \times \frac{2}{5}$
   c $\frac{2}{3} \div \frac{2}{9}$
   d $\frac{3}{4} + \frac{1}{5}$
   e $\frac{1}{2} + \frac{5}{12}$
   f $\frac{5}{6} \times \frac{2}{3}$

8. Alan calculates $15 \times \frac{2}{3}$ and gets the answer $\frac{30}{45}$.
   What mistake has he made and what is the correct answer?

9. Neil makes 2.75 kg of jam.
   He puts the jam into glass jars that contain a maximum of 350 g.
   a How many jars can he fill with the jam?

   Neil plans to sell the jam.
   He buys a pack of 10 glass jars for £3.
   The ingredients for the jam cost him £7.85 altogether.
   b For how much should he sell each jar of jam so that he will make a profit?

Calculator skills and formulae

You should learn to use the keys on your own calculator.
They may be different from the ones shown here: Try these for yourself:

To **square** a number, press the x^2 key   `3` x^2 `=`   You should get 9.

To **cube** a number, press the x^3 key   `4` x^3 `=`   You should get 64.

To **square root** a number, press the $\sqrt{}$ key $\sqrt{}$ `4` `=`   You should get 2.

To **cube root** a number, press the $\sqrt[3]{}$ key   `SHIFT` x^3 `2` `7` `=`   You should get 3.

On a calculator, negative numbers are often entered using the `(−)` key.

The cube root is often above the $\sqrt{}$ key

You should put brackets around negative numbers in a formula.

EXAMPLE

1 Find the value of   **a** $\dfrac{4.5}{\sqrt{13.7 - 2.4^2}}$ **b** $\sqrt[3]{32 + (-5.1)^2}$

and round each answer to 2 sf.

2 The formula for the volume of a cone is $V = \dfrac{\pi r^2 h}{3}$.
Find the volume of a cone, in m³, with $r = 45$ cm and $h = 1.2$ m.

The first bracket after $\sqrt{}$ appears automatically for some calculators.

---

1 **a** `4.5` `÷` `(` `√` `(` `13.7` `−` `2.4` x^2 `)` `)` = 1.596990… = **1.6 to 2 sf**
   b $\sqrt[3]{}$ `(` `32` `+` `(` `(−)` `5.1` `)` x^2 `)` = 3.8710990… = **3.9 to 2 sf**

Change cm to m

Always write more than 2sf and then round the answer.

2   $V = \dfrac{\pi \times 0.45^2 \times 1.2}{3}$

    = `(` `π` `×` `.45` x^2 `×` `1.2` `)` `÷` `3` = 0.254469… = **0.25 to 2 sf**

Use the π key or 3.142

The information is to 2sf so it is sensible to round the answer to 2sf.

You should also be careful when entering negative values into an equation.

EXAMPLE

Complete the table of values for $y = 3x^2 - 2x$.

x	−3	−2	−1	0
$3x^2 - 2x$		16		0

When $x = -3$, $3x^2 - 2x = 3 \times (-3)^2 - 2 \times -3 = 33$
When $x = -1$, $3x^2 - 2x = 3 \times (-1)^2 - 2 \times -1 = 5$

x	−3	−2	−1	0
$3x^2 - 2x$	33	16	5	0

Check your method by using $x = -2$. If you get 16 you are probably doing the right thing.

Exercise CN2

MEDIUM

1 Calculate the value of each of the following.
   Give each answer correct to 3 sf.

   a $\dfrac{4.5 - 2.7}{3.2}$

   b $\sqrt{3.2^2 + 1.7^2}$

   c $\dfrac{\sqrt{37.9}}{2.4^2}$

   d $\dfrac{12.7 - 3.6^2}{2.1 + 5}$

   e $\sqrt[3]{63.3 - 2.4^2}$

   f $32.4 - \dfrac{127}{2.3^2}$

   g $(-4.5)^3 + \sqrt{27}$

   h $\left(\dfrac{2}{1.3^3}\right)^2$

2 The area of a circle may be found using the formula $A = \pi r^2$.
   Calculate the area of a circle when $r = 39$ mm.
   Give your answer in cm².

3 Complete this table of values for $y = 5x^2 - x$.

x	−3	−2	−1	0	1
$5x^2 - x$	48			0	

4 The time it takes for a pendulum to complete one swing may be found using the formula
   $T = 2\pi\sqrt{\dfrac{l}{g}}$.

   Find the time for a pendulum to complete one swing when $l = 13.7$ and $g = 10.8$.

5 Find the values of the following expressions.

   a $x^3 - 2$ when $x = 5.1$

   b $\dfrac{a + ab}{6}$ when $a = 5$ and $b = -2$

   c $\sqrt{p^2 - q^2}$ when $p = 13.2$ and $q = 1.6$

   d $3x^3 - 4y^2$ when $x = 1.8$ and $y = -2$

   e $\dfrac{\pi r^2 h}{3}$ when $r = 4.5$ cm and $h = 12$ mm

6 Complete this table of values for $y = 2 + 3x^2$.

x	−3	−2	−1	0	1
$2 + 3x^2$	29			2	

7 Use trial and improvement to find a value of x so that $3x^3 - x = 20$ to 1 dp.
   Start with $x = 2$ and show all your working like this.
   $x = 2$ $3 \times 2^3 - 2 = ...$

Percentage problems

	Step 1	Step 2	Step 3
To find **P**% of amount **Q** →	Divide **P** by 100 →	multiply by **Q**	
To **increase** amount **Q** by **P**% →	Add **P** to 100 →	divide by 100 →	multiply by **Q**
To **decrease** amount **Q** by **P**% →	Take **P** from 100 →	divide by 100 →	multiply by **Q**

You can use these methods to repeatedly change an amount by a percentage.

EXAMPLE

A plant grows in height by 23% each year.
At the end of a year it is 85 cm high.
Find its height after 4 more years.

Step 1 $100 + 23 = 123$
Step 2 $123 \div 100 = 1.23$
Step 3 $85 \times 1.23 \times 1.23 \times 1.23 \times 1.23 =$
             $194.55364\ldots = 194.6$ cm to 1 dp

> $1.23 \times 1.23 \times 1.23 \times 1.23$ is the same as 1.23^4
> Do this on the calculator as 1.23 [$x^{\blacksquare}$] 4
> This is **much** quicker than finding 23%, adding it on then finding another 23% etc.

EXAMPLE

a   Find 27% of 2.39 m correct to 2 dp.
b   Barry's weekly train fare increases by 11.5%.
    He used to pay £35.60 a week.
    Calculate the cost of his new weekly fare.
c   Chloe has £2300 to invest.
    Her bank offers her 4.5% interest each year, which will be added to her savings.
    How much will Chloe's savings be worth at the end of 5 years and how much interest will she have?
d   A human being loses around 1.5% of their height every 10 years once they are older than 40.
    After 70 the percentage may be bigger.
    Jonah is 180 cm tall on his fortieth birthday.
    How tall could he expect to be on his sixtieth birthday?
e   Rory buys a pair of trainers for £85 but they rub his feet.
    He sells them for £70.
    What is his percentage loss?

← **LOOK BACK**
See topic AN1 to revise multiplying and dividing by powers of 10.

> This is called **compound interest**.

> It is a good idea to write £ in the calculation to help you remember the units (£) for the answer.
> Round to the nearest penny.

a 0.27×2.39 m $= 0.6453 = 0.65$ m to 2 dp
b $1.115 \times £35.60 = £39.694 = £39.69$
c $1.045^5 \times £2300 = £2866.2184\ldots = £2866.22$
    She earned $£2866.22 - 2300 = £566.22$ interest.
d $0.985^2 \times 180 = 174.6405 = 175$ cm
e $15 \div 85 \times 100 = 17.647\ldots = 17.6\%$ to 1 dp

> Step 1 $100 - 1.5 = 98.5$
> Step 2 $98.5 \div 100 = 0.985$
> There are two lots of ten years from 40 to 60 so 0.985^2

> He loses £15 so he has lost $\frac{15}{85}$ of the money he spent.
> Always divide by the original amount.

Exercise CN3

 MEDIUM

1. Write down the calculation needed to find each of the following.
   Then work out the answers and round the answer sensibly, when needed.
   - a 25% of £24.60
   - b 7% of 42 km
   - c 11% of 12 kg
   - d 17.5% of 49.8 m
   - e 22.5% of 8 hours
   - f 1% of 46p

2. A design has an area of 150 cm^2.
   It is photocopied and the area is enlarged by 12%.
   What is the area of the enlarged design?

3. Sally bought an old bike for £32.
   She repaired it and sold it for £44.
   What was her percentage profit?

4. Karen's salary, before any deductions, is £1455 a month.
   She is given a pay rise of 7.5%.
   - a Calculate her new monthly pay.
   - b Karen has 17% of her new salary deducted for tax.
     Calculate how much money Karen is actually paid.

5. Kevin used to weigh 165 pounds but, after a diet, he weighed 145 pounds.
   What was his percentage weight loss?

6. For an average man aged between 17 and 29, 8% of body weight is fat.
   - a Tony weighs 75 kg on his 28th birthday.
     Calculate how much of Tony's weight is fat.
   - b Tony is not very fit and gains weight by 5% each year.
     Calculate Tony's possible body weight on his 35th birthday.
   - c Explain why he may not weigh this amount on his 35th birthday.

7. The value of a car decreases at the rate of 15% each year for the first 3 years.
   A new car is bought for £10 500. Calculate the value of the car after three years.

8. At the start of 2010 the average house price was £224 000.
   It is predicted that house prices will rise by 2% each year.
   - a What will the average house price be at the start of 2020?
   - b Explain why this may not be the average house price in 2020.

9. Joan has £2600 to invest.
   She can either,
   - a buy a bond that pays 4.8% compound interest each year but
     she cannot take out any of the money until 5 years have passed, or
   - b have a savings account that pays 5% of £2600 each year.

   Which account would you recommend to Joan and why would you recommend it?

Percentage problems

Bounds of measurement

An instrument is only as accurate as the scale marked on it.

If you use a ruler marked in centimetres, you will always measure to the **nearest mark on the scale**.

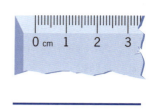

The three blue lines are all measured as 3 cm to the nearest cm.
However they are all different lengths.
Measurement gives an error of 0.5 cm either way (±0.5 cm).

EXAMPLE

a A boy is weighed as 64 kg, correct to the nearest kg.
 What is his least possible weight?
b A greetings card is 15 cm long, correct to the nearest cm.
 An envelope is 14.5 cm long correct to the nearest mm.
 Explain whether the card could ever fit into the envelope.
c A building is 800 m tall, correct to the nearest 10 m.
 What is the maximum possible height of the building?

a 63.5 kg ← There is an 'error' of 0.5 kg, so 64 − 0.5 = 63.5
b The card, recorded as 15 cm, could be as long as 14.5 cm.
 The envelope, recorded as 145 mm, could be as short
 as 144.5 mm (or 14.45 cm). ← Change 14.5 cm to mm and add half a mm.
 So the card could be shorter than the envelope
 and so fit inside it.
c 1400 + 50 = 1450 ← Because the building is measured to the nearest 10m, there is an 'error' of 5m.
 The maximum height of the building is 1450 m.

Exercise CN4

MEDIUM

1 A fish is weighed as 2.5 kg, correct to the nearest 100 g.
 What are the lowest and highest weights the fish could have?

2 On a plan, a room is shown as 250 cm wide and 460 cm long, each correct to the nearest 10 cm.
 Ken has a carpet that is exactly 240 cm wide and 470 cm long.
 Will the carpet fit in the room?

3 The world record for a height jumped by a horse is 2.18 m.
 Jo jumped 2.2 m, correct to the nearest 10 cm.
 Is it certain that Jo beat the world record?

4 The world's tallest building, the Burj Khalifa in Dubai, is 828 metres tall.
 It is not clear whether this is exact or rounded to some unit.
 a Show the different maximum heights if the measurement is rounded
  i to the nearest m
  ii to the nearest half m
  iii to the nearest cm.
 b Which rounding records the greatest height for the building?

Proportion

CN5

You use **proportion** in problems where amounts are scaled up or down by multiplying or dividing.

EXAMPLE

a A bag of biscuits weighs 250 g and costs £1.70.
   How much will a bag weighing 300 g cost?

b Choco Pops costs £1.75 for 350 g.
   Choc Rice costs £1.90 for 400 g.
   Which cereal is better 'value for money'?

c It is thought that 4 monks took 5 years to copy an ancient manuscript.
   How long would it have taken
   i   1 monk
   ii 10 monks to complete this task?

Change the cost to pence to avoid very small answers.

Work out the cost of 1 g as this is easy to 'scale up' to 300 g.

a 1 g costs 170p ÷ 250 = 0.68p
   300 g costs 0.68p × 300 = 204p or £2.04

b 50 g of Choco Pops costs   175p ÷ 7 = 25p
   50g of Choc Rice costs   190p ÷ 8 = 23.75p
   Choc Rice is best value.

350 ÷ 50 = 7
400 ÷ 50 = 8

c i   4 × 5 = 20 years
   ii 20 ÷ 10 = 2 years

Do a reality check:
It takes one monk MUCH longer working on his own so this is a multiplication.

Many hands make quicker work so this is a division.

Exercise CN5

MEDIUM

1 Brian walks 10 km in four hours. How far, at the same pace, will he walk in 10 hours?

2 One portion of cereal, weighing 30 g, contains 173 kcal.
   The recommended daily amount for a woman is 2000 kcal.
   A box contains 375 g of cereal.
   Tina eats half the box of cereal.
   Has she eaten her recommended daily amount of kcal?

3 These are some of the ingredients for making 10 chocolate muffins.
   a How much of each ingredient would you need to make 25 of these muffins?
   b Why would it be difficult to make a number of muffins that was not a multiple of 5, using this recipe?

Recipe

115 g butter at room temperature

70 g caster sugar

2 eggs at room temperature

215 g plain flour

4 It takes 5 workers 6 hours to harvest a field.
   One worker hurts his back and has to go home.
   How long will it take the remaining workers to harvest the next field, which is twice as big as the last one?

Compound measures   CN6

Compound measures involve two units, for example
- **Speed** measured in mph or miles per hour (the distance you travel in one hour)
- **Density** measured in g/cm³ or grams per cm³ (the weight of one cm³ of the material)

The units of density are g/cm³.

g is a measure of **mass**, cm³ is a measure of **volume** and / is divide.

So density = $\dfrac{\text{mass}}{\text{volume}}$

You can use 'cover up' to turn this into three formulae.

So density = $\dfrac{\text{mass}}{\text{volume}}$ volume = $\dfrac{\text{mass}}{\text{density}}$

and mass = density × volume

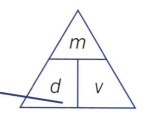

EXAMPLE

a Brian cycles at a steady speed of 12 km/h.
How far will he cycle in 45 minutes?

b Maryann is paid £15.30 per hour.
For how long will she have to work to earn £210?

c At the end of 2008:
The UK had a population of 61 414 000. The area of the UK is 244 820 square miles.
China had a population of 1 321 000 000. The area of China is 24 576 000 square miles.
Which country was most densely populated at the end of 2008?

d Dain is paid 45p to address 10 envelopes.
It takes him 5 minutes to address 15 envelopes.
If Dain works at the same pace for 3 hours, how much money will he earn?

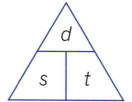

---

a You are asked for distance:

$d = s \times t = 12 \times \dfrac{3}{4} = 9$ km.

(45 minutes = $\dfrac{3}{4}$ h)

b 210 ÷ 15.3 = 13.725... hrs

Maryann will have to work for 14 hours.

(She can only work 13 or 14, and 13 is not enough!)

c Population density = $\dfrac{\text{population}}{\text{area}}$

UK = $\dfrac{61\,414\,000 \text{ people}}{244\,820 \text{ miles}^2}$ = 250.853... ≈ 251 people per square mile

China = $\dfrac{1\,321\,000\,000 \text{ people}}{24\,576\,000 \text{ miles}^2}$ = 53.75... ≈ 54 people per square mile

The UK was most densely populated (roughly 5 times greater than China).

d In 1 hour   60 ÷ 5 = 12 lots of 15 envelopes
            = 180 envelopes

In 3 hours   = 180 × 3 = 540 envelopes.

540 ÷ 10 = 54 lots of 10 envelopes

Dain is paid 54 × 45p = 2430p

= £24.30 in 3 hours.

(Keep pence in the calculation to avoid silly answers like £2430.)

Exercise CN6

1. What is the average speed of a cyclist who travels 30 km in $1\frac{1}{2}$ hours?

2. A car travels for 1 hour 45 minutes at a steady speed of 60 km/h.
   How far has the car travelled?

3. Sue walks from home to the shops at a steady 3 mph.
   The shops are 2 miles from home.
   How many minutes does the walk take Sue?

4. Silver has a density of 10.5 g/cm³. A silver bracelet weighs 200 g.
   a   How many cm³ of silver have been used to make the bracelet?

   The cost of the silver used to make the bracelet is £1762.
   b   What is the cost of 1 g of silver?

5. The cost of a single text message is 12p.
   However, you can buy a package of 30 messages at £3 per month.
   Give an example to show the following (think about what they use their phone for and whether they text a lot).
   a   Someone who is better off sending single text messages.
   b   Someone who is better off buying a package of messages.

6. A Cape Hunting Dog can run at a speed of 45 mph.
   At this speed, how far will it run in 3 minutes?

7. Colin cleans windows. He uses this information to estimate his income.

Large house	1 house every 18 minutes	
Average house	1 house every 8 minutes	£12
Small house	1 house every 6 minutes	

   How much should he charge for each other type of house?

8. A photocopier will print 110 copies per minute.
   How long will it take to print 20 documents each containing 440 pages?

9. Water from a tap flows at a rate of 12.5 cm³ per second.
   The tap fills a container in 11.6 seconds.
   a   What is the volume of the container?
   b   The same tap fills another container in 0.5 minutes.
       What is the volume of this container?
   c   The same tap is used to fill a 1 litre container.
       How many minutes will it take to do this?

3D coordinates

CA1

- 3D coordinates are used to represent points in space. The coordinate directions are *x*, *y* and *z*.

The point $P(2, 5, -4)$ is located +2 units in the *x* direction, +5 in the *y* direction, and −4 in the *z* direction.

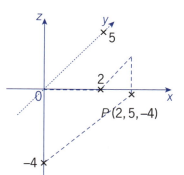

EXAMPLE

The cuboid *OABCDEFG* has one vertex at the point (5, 3, 2).

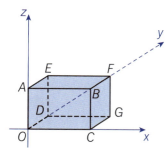

Write down the coordinates of
- **a** point *A*
- **b** point *G*
- **c** the midpoint of *OF*

Looking at the diagram, the point *F* must be at (5, 3, 2) because other points would have at least one zero in their coordinates.
- **a** *A* is (0, 0, 2)
- **b** *G* is (5, 3, 0)
- **c** The midpoint of (0, 0, 0) and (5, 3, 2) is (2.5, 1.5, 1).

To find the midpoint, take the (mean) average of each of the three coordinates.

Exercise CA1

MEDIUM

1. An archeological dig is taking place in a field.
   The archaeologists use a coordinate system where each unit represents 1 metre.

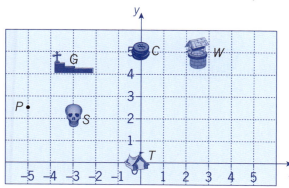

   - **a** The flag on the tent, T, is 5 m above ground level. Give the 3D coordinates of the flag.
   - **b** The skull, S, is found 1 m below ground level. Give the 3D coordinates of the skull.
   - **c** The coins, C, are found at ground level. Give the 3D coordinates of the coins.
   - **d** The bottom of the grave, G, is 2 m deep. Give the 3D coordinates of the centre of the base of the grave.
   - **e** The well, W, is 18 m deep. Give the 3D coordinates of the centre of bottom of the well.
   - **f** A retaining rope is attached from the top of the flagpole to ground level at *P*. Give the 3D coordinates of the centre of the rope.

Trial and improvement

CA2

- **Trial and improvement** is a method of solving equations where there is no simple algebraic solution.

← **LOOK BACK**
See topic AA1 to revise the use of symbols.

EXAMPLE

a Show that the equation $x^3 - 2x = 15$ has a solution between 2 and 3.

b Use trial and improvement to find this solution correct to 2 decimal places. Show all your **trials** and their outcomes.

A **trial** occurs when you substitute a value into the equation.

a When $x = 2$, $x^3 - 2x = 2^3 - 2 \times 2$
$= 8 - 4$
$= 4$

When $x = 3$, $x^3 - 2x = 3^3 - 2 \times 3$
$= 27 - 6$
$= 21$

Because the first value is **less** than 15 and the second is **greater** than 15, the solution must lie between these two values.

b Put your results in a table:

x	$x^3 - 2x$	Comment
2.4	9.024	Too small
2.7	14.283	Too small
2.8	16.352	Too big
2.73	14.886 417	Too small
2.74	15.090 824 0	Too big
2.735	14.988 415 4	Too small

Because the solution lies between 2.735 and 2.74, $x = 2.74$ to 2 decimal places.

It doesn't matter how many different values you try.

EXAMINER'S TIP
You must do the halfway value to confirm whether 2.73 or 2.74 is closest. Otherwise you will lose marks.

Exercise CA2

— MEDIUM

1 Use trial and improvement to solve these equations, giving your answer correct to 1 decimal place.
  a $x^3 + x = 20$
  b $2x^3 - x = 10$
  c $4x - x^3 = -16$
  d $2^x = 11$
  e $5^x = 20$
  f $3^x = 0.8$

2 Use trial and improvement to solve these equations, giving your answer correct to 2 decimal places.
  a $x^3 - 5x = 5$
  b $6^x + x = 30$
  c $6x^2 - x^5 = 8$

3 A cuboid of volume 100 cm³ has its length 1 cm more than its width. Its height is 1 cm more than its length. Its width is given by w.
  a Explain why $w(w + 1)(w + 2) = 100$.
  b Show that $3 < w < 4$.
  c Use trial and improvement to find w correct to 3 decimal places.

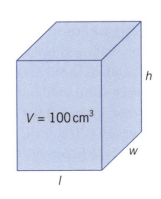

Graphs from real life

CA3

You need to be able to construct and interpret graphs from real life.

EXAMPLE

This sketch graph shows how much Jayne pays for her gas depending on what volume she uses.

Describe what the different sections of the graph represent.

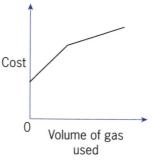

→ **LOOK BACK**
See Topic AA3 to revise formulae.

Because the graph doesn't start at the origin, there is a fixed standing charge. The first straight-line section represents a fixed charge per unit volume. The second section has a smaller gradient, so it represents a **lower** fixed charge per unit volume.

Exercise CA3

MEDIUM

1 Sketch a graph to illustrate each of these situations:
   a the temperature of a cup of coffee over a half-hour period
   b the cost of heating a house over a year
   c the speed of a parachutist after she jumps from a plane
   d the level of water in a full sink after the plug is pulled.

2 The graph shows Adam's journey from home to his swimming lesson.
   He walks to the bus stop and then gets the bus to the swimming pool 7 miles from home.
   At the pool he waits for 10 minutes and then has a 45-minute lesson.
   His mother picks him up from the pool and drives him home in her car, a journey that takes 10 minutes.

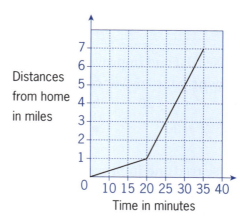

   a Copy and complete the distance–time graph. You will need to extend the x-axis.
   b Calculate the average speed for each of the three parts of Adam's journey: walking, bus and car.
   c What feature **of the graph** shows that the bus journey is faster than the walking section?
   d Describe two ways in which this graph is not an accurate representation of what happens in real life.

Graphs of quadratic functions — CA4

- A **quadratic function** has a squared term as its highest power. $y = x^2$ and $y = 3x^2 + 4$ are quadratic functions.

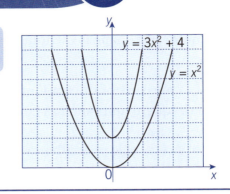

Graphs of quadratic functions have a distinctive **parabolic** shape.
These graphs can be used to find approximate solutions to **quadratic equations**.

EXAMPLE

a Complete this table of values and draw the graph of $y = 2x^2 - 3$.

x	-2	-1.5	-1	-0.5	0	0.5	1	1.5	2
y	5	1.5		-2.5		-2.5		1.5	5

b Use your graph to solve $2x^2 - 3 = 0$.

c Use your graph to solve $2x^2 - 3 = -2$.

---

a When $x = -1$, $y = 2 \times (-1)^2 - 3$
$\qquad\qquad\qquad = -1$
When $x = 0$, $y = 2 \times (0)^2 - 3$
$\qquad\qquad\qquad = -3$
When $x = 1$, $y = 2 \times 1^2 - 3$
$\qquad\qquad\qquad = -1$

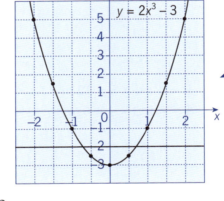

Quadratic graphs always look like ∪ or ∩.

b $2x^2 - 3 = 0$
So the solutions are where the graph crosses the line $y = 0$, that is the x-axis. Therefore the solutions are $x = -1.2$ and $x = 1.2$

c $2x^2 - 3 = -2$
So the solutions are where the graph crosses the line $y = -2$.

Exercise CA4 — MEDIUM

1 Draw the graphs of these functions for $-3 \leq x \leq 3$.
  a $y = x^2 - 2$
  b $y = x^2 + 3$
  c $y = x^2 - 5$
  d $y = 2x^2 - 1$
  e $y = 2x^2 - 3$
  f $y = 3x^2 - 7$
  g $y = 10 - x^2$
  h $y = 2 - x^2$

2 Use your graphs from Question **1** to write approximate solutions to these equations.
  a $x^2 - 2 = 0$
  b $x^2 + 3 = 8$
  c $x^2 - 5 = 5$
  d $2x^2 - 1 = 0$
  e $2x^2 - 3 = 15$
  f $3x^2 - 7 = -2$
  g $10 - x^2 = 6$
  h $2 - x^2 = -3$

3 Look at the graph of $y = 3x^2 - 7$ in Question **1f**. If the equation $3x^2 - 7 = k$ has no solutions, what can you say about k?

EXAMINER'S TIP
There are usually (but not always) two solutions to a quadratic equation — don't forget to write both of them.

Perimeter and area of basic shapes

The **perimeter** of a shape is the total distance around its edge. It is a length.

The **area** is a measure of the amount of space enclosed and is measured in square units such as cm².

← **LOOK BACK**
See Topic AG1 to revise measurements and scale.

- Area of a rectangle = length × width = lw
  Calculations must be done using the same units.
- Area of triangle = $\frac{1}{2}$ × base × perpendicular height
  $= \frac{1}{2}bh = \frac{bh}{2}$

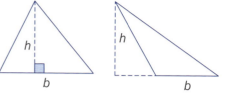

EXAMPLE

Find the perimeter and area of the following shapes.

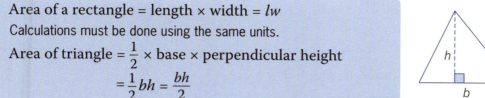

a $P = 2 \times 3 + 2 \times 7$
   $= 6 + 14 = 20\,\text{cm}$
   $A = 3 \times 7 = 21\,\text{cm}^2$

b $P = 3 + 4 + 5 = 12\,\text{m}$
   $A = \frac{1}{2} \times 3 \times 4 = 6\,\text{m}^2$

c $P = 2 \times 13 + 10$
   $= 26 + 10 = 36\,\text{units}$
   $A = \frac{1}{2} \times 10 \times 12 = 60\,\text{unit}^2$

More complicated (called **composite**) shapes can be broken down into simple shapes to calculate their areas.

EXAMPLE

Find the area of the following shape:

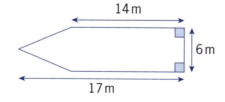

Area = triangle + rectangle = $\frac{1}{2} \times 6 \times 3 + 6 \times 14$
$= 9 + 84 = 93\,\text{m}^2$

Break the shape down into two pieces:

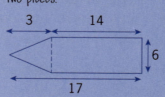

EXAMPLE

Fergus decides to put a new carpet in his front room. He draws a plan of the room and measures the dimensions of the room carefully. The carpet he wishes to use costs £6.40 per square metre. Find the total cost of carpeting his room.

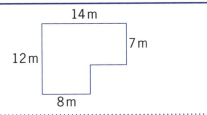

Method 1: divide into two rectangles

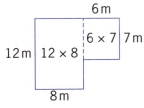

Method 2: subtract small rectangle from large

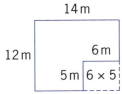

$A = 8 \times 12 + 7 \times 6 = 138 \, m^2$

$A = 14 \times 12 - 5 \times 6 = 138 \, m^2$

Whichever method is used the total cost $= 138 \times 6.4 = £883.20$.

Exercise CG1   **MEDIUM**

1. By measuring suitable lengths, find the perimeter and area of the following shapes. Make sure you give the units of your answer clearly.

   a    b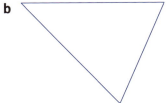

2. Calculate the area of the following shapes:

   a 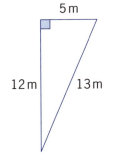   b 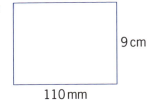   c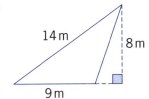

3. A rectangle has a perimeter of 26 cm. Its width is 4 cm. Find its area.

4. Plot the points $O(0,0)$, $A(4,0)$, $B(4,3)$ and $C(2,3)$ on a coordinate grid and find the area of the resultant shape $OABC$.

5. Find the area of this composite shape. Show your method carefully.

   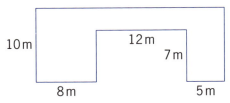

6. A farmer's field is shown. The scale for the sketch is 1 cm = 100 m.
   a. Find the approximate area of the field in square metres.
   b. Given that 1 hectare = 10 000 m² find the area of the field in hectares.
   c. Fertiliser costs £250 per tonne. One hectare requires 40 kg of fertiliser. What is the cost of fertiliser to cover the whole field?

   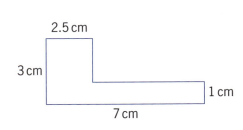

Perimeter and area of basic shapes

Circumference and area of circles CG2

If you know the radius or diameter you can use π (pronounced "pi") to find the circumference and area of a circle.

You can use your calculator value for π though it is approximately 3.142 or $\frac{22}{7}$.

- Circumference (perimeter) of circle $C = \pi \times d = \pi d = 2\pi r$
- Circumference is a length so is measured in cm, m, ...
  Area is measured in cm^2, m^2 ...
- Area of circle $A = \pi \times r^2 = \pi r^2$

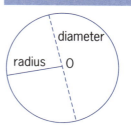

EXAMPLE

Find the circumference and area of a circle of diameter 4.2 m.

$C = \pi d = \pi \times 4.2 = 13.1946... = 13.2$ m (3 sf)
$A = \pi r^2 = \pi \times 2.1^2 = 13.8544... = 13.9$ m^2 (3 sf)

Units don't have to be put in until the final answer.

Halve the diameter to give the radius.

EXAMPLE

Find the circumference and area of a circle of radius 6 cm, leaving your answer in exact form.

No calculator is needed for this problem!

$C = 2\pi r = 2 \times \pi \times 6 = 12\pi$ cm $A = \pi r^2 = \pi \times 6^2 = 36\pi$ cm^2

EXAMPLE

The diameters of the wheels of a bicycle are 80 cm.
a Find the circumference of a wheel.
b A wheel turns 200 times. How far has the wheel travelled in metres?
c Mike wants to cycle 4 km. How many times does his front wheel turn around?

a $C = \pi \times d = \pi \times 80 = 251.327... = 251$ cm (3 sf)
b $200 \times 251.327... = 50\,265.482\,46$ cm $= 503$ m (3 sf)
c 4 km = 4000 m = 400 000 cm, 400 000 ÷ (π × 80) = 1591.549... ≈ 1592 times

EXAMPLE

Daud has designed a door for the front of his house.
Here is the plan.
He buys a rectangle of wood with dimensions 1.9 m × 0.9 m.
How much wood will he waste in making his door?

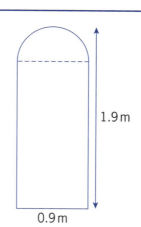

The door can be seen as a rectangle plus a semicircle.
Area of rectangle $= 0.9 \times (1.9 - 0.45) = 1.305$ m^2
Area of semicircle $\pi \times 0.45^2 \div 2 = 0.31808...$ m^2
Total area of door $= 1.623$ m^2
Wood wasted $= 1.9 \times 0.9 - 1.623 = 0.087$ m^2 (3 dp)

Exercise CG2

MEDIUM

Ensure you show all relevant working and units of measurement.
Give your answers to 3 significant figures where appropriate.

1. By making a suitable measurement, find the circumference and area of this circle.

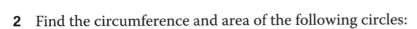

2. Find the circumference and area of the following circles:
   a radius 4 m
   b diameter 40.8 cm

3. Find the area of the shaded regions in the following.
   a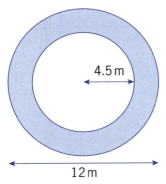
   b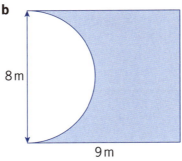

4. A car wheel has radius 40 cm.
   a Find the circumference of the wheel.
   b How far has the car travelled if the wheel has rotated fully 4000 times?
   Give your answer in suitable units.

5. A semicircular garden display has diameter 4 m.
   a It costs £1.30 for each square metre of soil, laid 5 cm deep.
   How much does it cost to fully cover the semicircular garden?
   b There is a wood edging to enclose the garden.
   The wood costs £3.50 for each metre.
   How much does the edging cost?

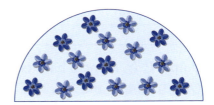

6. a Find the area of this badge.

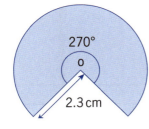

   b If the badge is made of silver and silver costs £65 per square cm then how much will the badge cost to make?

Area of parallelograms and trapeziums

- Area of parallelogram = base × perpendicular height
- Area of trapezium = $\frac{1}{2}$ × (sum of parallel sides) × perpendicular height
  $= \frac{1}{2} \times (a + b) \times h = \frac{1}{2}(a + b)h$

Perpendicular height of a trapezium is the distance between parallel sides.

Parallelogram

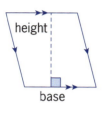 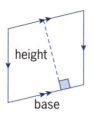 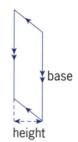

Trapezium

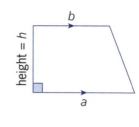 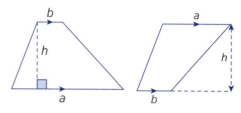

EXAMPLE

Find the area of the following shapes.

a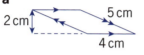
b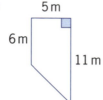
c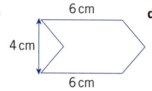
d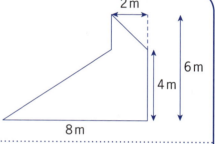

a Area = 4 × 2 = 8 cm²
b Area = $\frac{1}{2}$ (6 + 11) × 5 = 42.5 m²
c Area of one parallelogram = 6 × 2 = 12 cm² so total area = 2 × 12 = 24 cm²
d Area = area of trapezium + area of triangle = $\frac{1}{2}(8 + 2) \times 4 + \frac{1}{2} \times 2 \times 2 = 20 + 2 = 22$ m²

EXAMPLE

Points P, Q, R and S have coordinates $P(3,0)$, $Q(5,0)$, $R(4,3)$ and $S(1,3)$. Calculate the area of the trapezium $PQRS$.

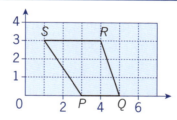

The parallel sides are PQ and SR so $a = 2$, $b = 3$ and $h = 3$
Area = $\frac{1}{2} \times (2 + 3) \times 3 = 7.5$ unit²

EXAMPLE

A modern art painting is hung in a school reception area. It is coloured white and blue as shown. Find the area of blue paint.

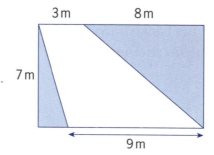

Area = area of rectangle − area of trapezium
= $7 \times 11 - \frac{1}{2} \times (3 + 9) \times 7 = 35$ m²

Area of parallelograms and trapeziums

Exercise CG3

MEDIUM

1. Find the area of these shapes. Give your answers in square units.

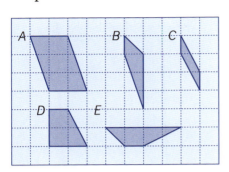

2. By taking appropriate measurements, find the area of the following shapes.

   a    b

3. Find the dimensions of a square which has the same area as this trapezium.

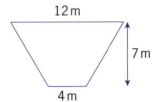

4. Plot the points $P(7,2)$, $Q(8,2)$, $R(5,4)$ and $S(1,4)$ and join them up in order to form a quadrilateral $PQRS$. Find the area of $PQRS$.

5. A path is shown shaded in the diagram. The path encloses a lawn.
   a Find the area of the lawn.
   b Over the years the path has become worn down so the owner decides to replace the paving slabs. A slab of $1\,m^2$ costs £8. How much will the owner need to spend to redo his path?

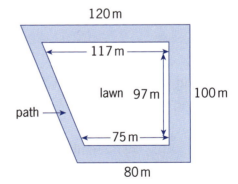

6. Draw sketches of three different trapeziums which each have an area of $60\,m^2$.

7. The design for a badge consists of two congruent parallelograms and two congruent trapeziums. It is to be covered in gold leaf which costs £16 per cm^2. Find the cost of covering the badge with gold leaf.

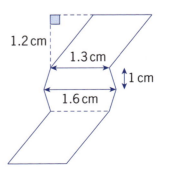

Area of parallelograms and trapeziums

Plans, elevations and nets CG4

Consider the following object:

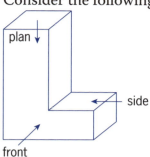

When you look at an object from above you get what is called a **plan view** or a bird's-eye view.

When you look at the object from the side you get what is called a **side elevation**.

When you look at an object from the front you see what is called a **front elevation**.

EXAMPLE

Given the plan view and front and side elevations for an object, sketch the original object.

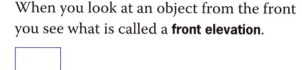

Be prepared to do a rough sketch and check your sketch against the three views given. It may take more than one attempt.

- A **net** is a 2D shape which can be folded to make a solid shape.

EXAMPLE

Draw the net for a square based pyramid.

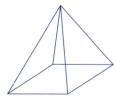

Sometimes there can be a number of different ways of drawing a net.

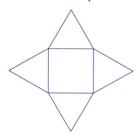

114 Plans, elevations and nets

EXAMPLE

What shapes are formed from the following nets?

a 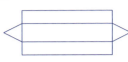   b

a triangular prism   b cube

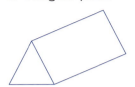

Exercise CG4

MEDIUM

1. Sketch the front and side elevations and the plan view for these shapes.

   a 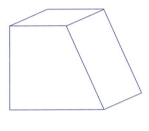   b 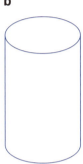   c

2. Given the plan view and elevations, sketch the whole object.

   plan view   side elevation   front elevation

3. Draw the elevations and plan view of these shapes.

   a   b
   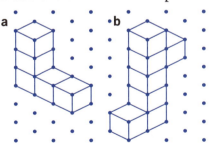

   *These shapes are drawn on an **isometric grid**.*

4. Sketch the nets of these shapes.

   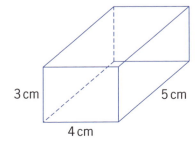   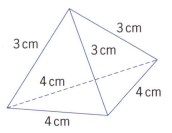

Plans, elevations and nets

Surface area and volume

CG5

- The **surface area** of a 3D object is the total area of its faces.

EXAMPLE

Find the surface area of this cuboid.

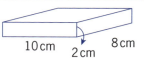
10 cm   2 cm   8 cm

The cuboid is made up of 6 faces, three pairs of which are identical.
$2 \times (10 \times 2) + 2 \times (8 \times 2) + 2 \times (8 \times 10)$
$= 40 + 32 + 160 = 232 \text{ cm}^2$

EXAMPLE

Here is the net of a square-based pyramid. The square has sides 6 cm and the height of each triangle is 4 cm. Find the surface area of the pyramid.

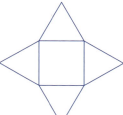

Area of square = $6 \times 6 = 36 \text{ cm}^2$
Area of one triangle = $\frac{1}{2} \times 6 \times 4 = 12 \text{ cm}^2$
Total area = $36 + 4 \times 12 = 84 \text{ cm}^2$

- A **prism** is a special type of object which has the same cross-section throughout its length.

Examples of prisms are cuboids, triangular prisms and cylinders.

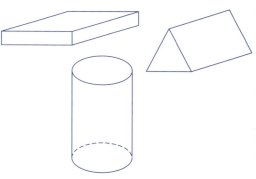

- The volume of a prism = area of cross-section × length
- The volume of a cylinder = area of circular end × height (length) of cylinder = $\pi r^2 \times h$
- The curved surface area of a cylinder = $2\pi rh$
- The total surface area of a **closed** cylinder = $2\pi rh + 2\pi r^2$

EXAMPLE

Find the volume of these prisms.

A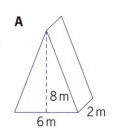
8 m, 6 m, 2 m

B 6 cm, 3 cm, 4 cm, 10 cm, 1 cm

A Area of cross-section = $\frac{1}{2} \times 6 \times 8 = 24 \text{ m}^2$
so volume = area × length = $24 \times 2 = 48 \text{ m}^3$

B Area of cross-section = $10 \times 6 - 7 \times 5 = 25 \text{ cm}^2$
so volume = area × length = $25 \times 4 = 100 \text{ cm}^3$

EXAMPLE

a How much concrete is required to make a large drainage pipe of length 20 m with internal radius 5 m and external radius 5.2 m?

b If 1 m³ of concrete weighs 300 kg, how much does the pipe weigh?

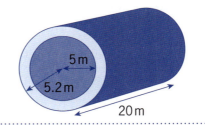

a Area of cross-section = π × 5.2² − π × 5² = 6.408849...
= 6.41 m² (3 sf)

so volume = area × length = 6.408849... × 20
= 128.176... = 128 m³ (3 sf)

b Weight of pipe = 128.176 ... × 300 = 38 453 kg
= 38.5 tonnes (3 sf)

Exercise CG5

MEDIUM

1 Find the surface area and volume of the following prisms. Show your method and give units in the final answers.

a   b   c   d

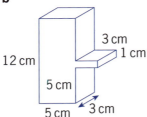 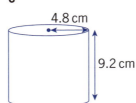 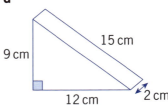

2 The diagram shows the cross-section of a swimming pool with width 8 m.
  a Find the volume of the swimming pool.
  b How many litres of water does it hold when full?
  c The pool is filled at a rate of 2 litres per second. How long does it take to fill the pool? Give your answer in appropriate units.

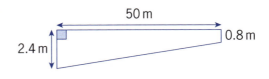

3 Using the diagram shown, explain carefully why the curved surface area of a cylinder is $2\pi rh$.

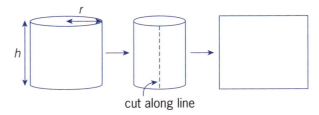

4 Find the volume and total surface area of a closed cylinder with base radius 5 cm and height 17 cm.

5 A child's wooden toy is in the shape of a house.
  a Find the volume of the house.
  b The wood is willow. 10 cm³ of willow weighs 4.2 g. How much does the toy weigh?

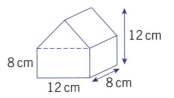

Surface area and volume

Length, area and volume scale

You should be able to work out these unit conversions:

$1\,cm = 10\,mm \qquad 1\,m = 100\,cm$
$1\,cm^2 = 10^2\,mm^2 = 100\,mm^2$
$1\,m^2 = 100^2\,cm^2 = 10\,000\,cm^2$
$1\,cm^3 = 10^3\,mm^3 = 1000\,mm^3$
$1\,m^3 = 100^3\,cm^3 = 1\,000\,000\,cm^3$

EXAMPLE

Convert:
a $12\,cm^2$ to mm^2
b $2200\,mm^2$ to cm^2
c $5.1\,m^3$ to cm^3
d $35\,000\,cm^2$ to m^2

a $12 \times 10^2 = 12 \times 100 = 1200\,mm^2$
b $2200 \div 100 = 22\,cm^2$
c $5.1 \times 100^3 = 5\,100\,000$
d $35\,000 \div 100^2 = 3.5\,m^2$

- If an enlargement has scale factor p then the perimeter scale factor is p.

EXAMPLE

Plot the points $P(1, 0)$, $Q(5, 0)$, $R(5, 2)$ and $S(1, 2)$.
Enlarge the rectangle $PQRS$ with scale factor 2 and centre of enlargement the origin.
Write the perimeter of the enlarged rectangle $P'Q'R'S'$ and compare with the perimeter of $PQRS$.
Calculate and compare the areas of the two rectangles.

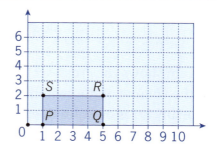

Perimeter of $PQRS$ = 12 units.
Perimeter of $P'Q'R'S'$ = 24 units.
Perimeter of $P'Q'R'S'$ = 2 × Perimeter of $PQRS$
Area of $PQRS$ = 8 unit^2 Area of $P'Q'R'S'$ = 32 unit^2
Area of $P'Q'R'S'$ = 4 × area of $PQRS$

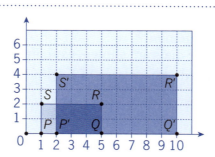

Exercise CG6

MEDIUM

1. Convert the following units to the units given in brackets:
   a $4\,cm^2$ (mm^2) b $9\,cm^3$ (mm^3) c $12\,000\,mm^2$ (cm^2) d $5\,km^2$ (m^2)
   e $7.3\,m^2$ (cm^2) f $3\,200\,000\,cm^3$ (m^3) g $435\,000\,000\,m^2$ (km^2)

2. Shape A has been enlarged by scale factor 2. What is the perimeter of the shape after the enlargement?

3. This triangle has been enlarged. Find the scale factor by working out the perimeter before and after the enlargement.

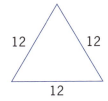

4. A star has perimeter 12. What will the perimeter be after an enlargement of scale factor 3?

P = 12

5. The perimeter of a rectangle after an enlargement of scale factor 4 is 20. What was the perimeter of the shape before the enlargement?

P = 20

6. Calculate the area of this symmetrical shape. If the lengths of this shape are increased by scale factor 4, calculate the area of the enlarged shape.

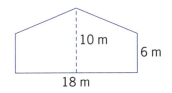

7. How many cubes of side 1 mm are required to fill a box with dimensions $20\,cm \times 10\,cm \times 8\,cm$?

Length, area and volume scale

Theoretical probability

CS1

Probability is a measure of how likely an outcome is to happen.
> Other probability words are 'likely' and 'unlikely'.

- An impossible outcome has probability 0.
- An outcome certain to happen has probability 1.
- All other possible outcomes have probabilities between 0 and 1.
- Probabilities are written as a fraction, decimal or percentage.

```
0              1/2              1
impossible    evens         certain
```

> If you have a probability answer greater than 1, check your calculation!

- Theoretical probability can be used when outcomes are equally likely.

$$\text{Theoretical probability} = \frac{\text{Number of ways the outcome can happen}}{\text{possible outcomes}}$$

> Use fractions when you can; recurring and rounded decimals are less precise.

EXAMPLE

A box contains five marbles.
The marbles are all the same size and shape.
Each marble is a different colour: purple, green, orange, white and yellow.
Lois chooses one marble at random from the box.
What is the probability that Lois chooses the white marble?

There are five possible outcomes.
Each outcome is equally likely.
Probability of each outcome = $\frac{1}{5}$
Probability of choosing white marble, P(white) = $\frac{1}{5}$

EXAMPLE

The letters of the word PROBABILITY are placed in a bag. Kim chooses one letter at random from the bag.

a Explain why the probability of choosing a vowel is less than $\frac{1}{2}$.

b What is the probability that Kim chooses
  i letter R   **ii** letter B?

a There are 11 letters altogether in the word PROBABILITY.
Four of these are vowels O, A, I and I.
P(vowel) = $\frac{4}{11}$ and $\frac{4}{11}$ is less than $\frac{1}{2}$.

> There are two letter I's.
> Both are included when finding probability.

b **i** P(letter R) = $\frac{1}{11}$

ii P(letter B) = $\frac{2}{11}$

Exercise CS1

MEDIUM LOW

1. A bag contains nine balls. Five are blue, two are red and two are yellow.
   Karen chooses a ball at random from the bag.
   a. What colours are equally likely to be chosen? Explain why.
   b. What is the probability that Karen chooses a red ball?

2. Simon and Sally like different types of music. Simon likes trance,
   Sally likes rock music. Together they have fifteen trance CDs and five rock CDs.
   One CD is chosen at random to play.
   The arrow on the scale shows the probability that the person
   choosing the CD likes the CD.
   Who chose the CD?

3. A spinner has eight equal sections.
   The spinner is spun once.
   a. What is the probability of scoring
      i. 3
      ii. an even number
      iii. a prime number?
   b. Design a spinner with 10 equal sections with these probabilities:
      P(score 1) = 0.5, P(score 2) = 0.3 and P(score 3) = 0.2

   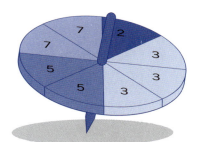

4. Amir rolls a fair dice. His score on the dice is 5.
   Sarah then rolls the same fair dice.
   What is the probability that she also scores 5?

5. A fair spinner has six equal sections.
   Three sections are red, two are blue and one is purple.
   a. There are only three colours and only one section is purple.
      Explain why the probability of purple is not $\frac{1}{3}$.
   b. The spinner is spun once.
      Write the probability that it lands on   i red   ii blue.

6. Joe has a six-sided dice. Each side has a different positive integer.
   Joe rolls the dice.
   The probability that he scores a multiple of four is 1.
   The probability that the score is less than six is 0.
   a. What is the lowest number that could be on the dice?

   The probability that he scores a number greater than 15 and less than 25 is $\frac{1}{2}$.
   b. Write any other numbers that you know are on the dice.

7. Mei has two bags of sweets. She can choose one sweet, without looking,
   from one of the bags.
   Bag A contains four cherry and five lime flavoured sweets.
   Bag B contains five cherry and five lime flavoured sweets.
   Mei likes the cherry sweets, but not the lime sweets.
   Which bag should Mei choose from?

Theoretical probability

Mutually exclusive events

CS2

- **Mutually exclusive** events cannot happen together.
- P(event E does not happen) = 1 − P(event E does happen)

EXAMPLE

Here is a spinner with eight equal sections.
The spinner is spun once.
What is the probability that the spinner lands on
a   white
b   not dark blue

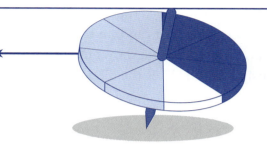

a Eight sections altogether, only one white
   $P(white) = \dfrac{1}{8}$

b Three sections are dark blue, eight sections altogether
   8 − 3 = 5
   so 5 are not dark blue and $P(dark\ blue) = \dfrac{5}{8}$

EXAMPLE

Jenny has a bag of sweets.
She chooses one sweet at random from the bag.
The probability that Jenny chooses a lime flavoured sweet = $\dfrac{1}{4}$.
Probability of choosing orange flavour = $\dfrac{3}{10}$
Probability of choosing blackcurrant flavour = $\dfrac{1}{6}$
Are there any other sweet flavours in the bag?
Explain your answer.

$\dfrac{1}{4} + \dfrac{3}{10} + \dfrac{1}{6} = \dfrac{15}{60} + \dfrac{18}{60} + \dfrac{10}{60} = \dfrac{43}{60} \neq 1$

If you know all the outcomes, add all their probabilities and their total should = 1

There must be other sweet flavours in the bag to make the total probability = 1

- The sum of all possible mutually exclusive outcomes is 1.

Mutually exclusive events

Exercise CS2

1. A fruit bowl contains 15 pieces of fruit: five apples, six bananas and four oranges. One piece of fruit is chosen at random.
   a What is the probability of choosing a banana?
   b What is the probability of choosing a fruit that is not an orange?

2. The probability that Matt arrives late for work on any day is 0.65.
   What is the probability that Matt is not late arriving for work?

3. There are some counters in a bag. They are either green or yellow.
   The probability that a green counter is chosen is $\frac{5}{9}$.
   a What is the probability of choosing a yellow counter?
   b What is the smallest number of yellow counters there could be in the bag?

4. There are 40 cars in a car park.
   Half the cars are silver, 12 are black and all the others are red.
   What is the probability that the next car to leave the car park is:
   a silver   b red   c not black?

5. I am going to take a cube from a large bag of cubes.
   The probability that the cube is black is $\frac{1}{8}$.
   a What is the probability that the cube is not black?
   There are four black cubes in the bag.
   b How many cubes are there in the bag altogether?

6. I have a large bag of lime, orange, blackcurrant and strawberry flavoured sweets and I choose one sweet at random.
   The table shows the probability of each flavour being chosen.

	Strawberry	Orange	Lime	Blackcurrant
Probability	x	0.4	0.15	0.25

   a What is the probability of choosing a lime or blackcurrant sweet?
   b What is the probability of choosing a strawberry flavoured sweet?

7. Mr Todd has a set of cards with different mathematics activities: either number, algebra, geometry or statistics.
   At the start of each week he chooses one card at random to use with a class.
   These are the probabilities of choosing a card for the different activities.

Mathematics	Number	Algebra	Geometry	Statistics
Probability	0.4	0.12	$3x$	x

   a How does the number of geometry activities compare to the number of statistics activities?
   b Work out the probability of choosing a statistics activity card.

Listing outcomes

CS3

When working out probability, you should list all possible outcomes systematically.
For two events you can use a table to record outcomes.

EXAMPLE

Five friends, Dee, Edith, Rashid, Gina and Harry, have just two tickets to go to a music festival. List all the possible ways that two of the five friends can go to the music festival together.

Dee and Edith
Dee and Rashid
Dee and Gina
Dee and Harry   Edith and Rashid
                  Edith and Gina
                  Edith and Harry   Rashid and Gina
                                      Rashid and Harry   Gina and Harry

Begin with one person, pair them up, then move on in order to the next person and pair up and continue.

EXAMPLE

Reuben has two strange four-sided dice.
One dice has the numbers 2, 3, 5 and −7.
The other dice has the numbers −2, −1, 1 and 3.
Reuben rolls both dice and multiplies their scores together.

a Draw a diagram to show all possible outcomes
b How many outcomes are there altogether?
c Find the probability that the outcome is
 i positive   **ii** a multiple of 3

a

×	2	3	5	−7
−2	−4	−6	−10	14
−1	−2	−3	−5	7
1	2	3	5	−7
3	6	9	15	−21

b There are 16 cells in the table, so there are 16 possible outcomes altogether.

c i There are 8 positive outcomes: 14, 7, 2, 3, 5, 6, 9 and 15.
$$P(\text{positive}) = \frac{8}{16} = \frac{1}{2}$$

  ii There are 7 multiples of 3: −6, −3, 3, 6, 9, 15 and −21.
$$P(\text{multiple of 3}) = \frac{7}{16}$$

Exercise CS3

MEDIUM

1. Four friends, Ann, Ben, Cas and Dee, are given just three cinema tickets. List all the different combinations of three friends that can go.

2. Jamal has two marbles, one purple and one orange.
   Peter has three marbles, one red, one purple and one green.
   They each choose one of their own marbles.

   a. Copy and complete the table to list the different ways in which the marbles might be chosen. Two entries have been completed for you.

		Peter		
		Red	Purple	Green
Jamal	Purple	P R	PP	
	Orange			

   b. What is the probability that Jamal and Peter both choose a purple marble?

3. Two spinners each have three equal sectors. Each spinner is spun and their scores are added to get a total score.

   a. Draw a table to show all possible total scores.
   b. What is the probability that the total is:
      i. 2   ii. 5   iii. greater than 5?

4. Two coins are spun.
   a. Write down all possible outcomes, in a list or in a table.
   b. Explain why the probability of getting a head and a tail is $\frac{1}{2}$.

5. Two ordinary fair dice, one blue and one white, are rolled together. Their scores are added to find the total score.
   a. Draw a table to show all possible total scores.
   b. How many possible outcomes are there?
   c. i. What is the most likely total score?
      ii. What is its probability?
   d. What is the probability of a total score of
      i. 12   ii. 5   iii. less than 5?

6. Two ordinary fair dice, one blue and one pink, are rolled together. The difference between their faces is found to find the score.
   a. Draw a table to show all possible scores.
   b. i. What is the most likely score?
      ii. What is its probability?
   c. What is the probability of a score of
      i. 1   ii. 2   iii. greater than 2?

7. Two ordinary fair dice, one red and one green, are rolled together. What is the probability that the score on the red dice is greater than or equal to the score on the green dice?

Listing outcomes

Experiments and relative frequency

You can **estimate probability** of an outcome by carrying out an **experiment**.
Use an experiment
- when theoretical probability is not possible
- when you want to test theoretical probability, for example to find out if a dice is biased.

> When there is no bias, experimental and theoretical probabilities will be very close but **not** exactly the same.
> Using decimals can help to make comparisons.

- **Relative frequency** or experimental probability = $\dfrac{\text{Number of successful trials}}{\text{Total number of trials}}$

The greater the number of trials, the more reliable the estimate of probability.

EXAMPLE

Zoe thinks she has a biased coin. She spins the coin many times and records, in batches of ten spins, the number of heads. These are her results.

Batch of ten spins	1st ten	2nd ten	3rd ten	4th ten
Number of heads	4	3	7	5

After the first 20 spins, Zoe says that the coin is biased.
After all 40 spins, Zoe is no longer sure if the coin is biased.
Explain how Zoe may have arrived at these conclusions.

With a fair coin P(head) = $\dfrac{1}{2}$ = 0.5

After 20 spins, relative frequency of head = $\dfrac{7}{20}$, $\dfrac{7}{20}$ = 0.35 is not close to 0.5

After 40 spins, relative frequency of head = $\dfrac{19}{40}$, $\dfrac{19}{40}$ = 0.475 is close to 0.5

EXAMPLE

A spinner has four coloured sections, red, blue, yellow and green.
Three students carried out an experiment to find out if the spinner was biased.
Here are their results.

Student	Number of spins	Red	Blue	Yellow	Green
Ann	70	22	16	18	14
Fadi	60	16	14	13	17
Carl	110	32	29	25	24

a Which student's data is most likely to be the most reliable? Explain your answer.

They collected all their results together in the following table.

Colour	Red	Blue	Yellow	Green
Frequency	70	59	56	55

b Do you think the spinner is biased? Explain your answer.
c What is the probability that the spinner lands on blue?

---

a Carl's, because he has carried out a lot more trials.
b Yes, biased to red as there is a lot more red than any other.
c P(blue) = $\dfrac{59}{240}$

Exercise CS4

1 Sheng-Li rolls a fair ordinary dice four times.
Her scores are 2, 6, 4 and 1.
Sheng-Li says that on her next roll of the dice she is sure to get either a 3 or a 5.
Is Sheng-Li correct? Explain your answer.

2 Julian spins an ordinary unbiased coin four times.
He gets tails, tails, tails, tails.
Julian says that it will impossible for him to get tails on the next spin of the coin.
Is Julian correct? Explain your answer.

3 A four-sided dice, numbered 1, 2, 3, 4, is rolled 300 times.
Here are the results.

Number on dice	1	2	3	4
Frequency	69	67	93	71

a Explain why the results suggest the dice may be biased.
b What is the probability of scoring a 3 on the next roll of the dice?

4 A spinner has ten equal sections. Each section has one colour.
The table summarises the results from 100 spins.

Colour	Red	Green	Orange	Yellow	Blue
Frequency	12	32	7	6	43

How many sections of each colour do you think there are? Explain your answer.

5 Four students carried out an experiment to see if a coin was biased.
Their results are summarised in the table.

	Donna	Ed	Freya	Gary
Heads	32	95	48	326
Tails	28	95	62	324

a Whose data is likely to give the most reliable answer to whether or not the coin is biased? Explain your answer.
b If they collect all their results together, how many tails would there be?
c Do you think the coin is biased or not? Explain your answer.

6 These are the scores from 20 throws of a dice.

5	2	3	3	1	6	5	3	4	2	5	6	4	3	1	2	4	5	6	1

a Is the dice biased towards any number? Explain your answer.
b Estimate the probability that on the next throw of the dice the score is 4.

GCSE formulae

In your OCR GCSE examinations you will be given a formula sheet.
Here are the formulae that you are given in your exams.

Area of a trapezium = $\frac{1}{2}(a + b)h$

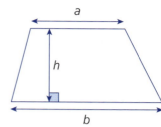

Volume of prism = area of cross section × length

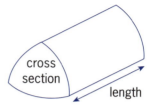

Here are some other formulae that you should learn.
Area of a rectangle = length × width

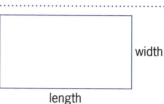

Area of a triangle = $\frac{1}{2}$ × base × height

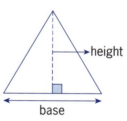

Area of a parallelogram = base × perpendicular height

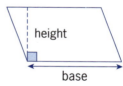

Area of a circle = πr^2
Circumference of a circle = $\pi d = 2\pi r$

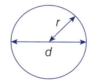

Volume of a cuboid = length × width × height

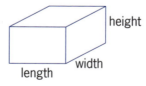

Volume of a cylinder = area of circle × length

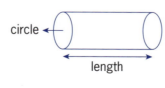

Pythagoras' theorem states,
For any right-angled triangle, $c^2 = a^2 + b^2$
where c is the hypotenuse.

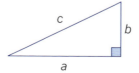

Unit A Foundation Practice Paper

60 marks   **1 hour**

1 This scoreboard shows Alan and Jamal's scores.
Alan slides the top pointers to show his score, Jamal slides the bottom one.

Alan | 0 | 1 | 2 | 3 | 4 | 5 | 6 | 7 | 8 | 9 | 10 | 11 | 12 | 13 | 14 | 15 | 16 | 17 | 18 | 19 | 0 | 20 | 40 | 60 | 80 | 100 |
Jamal

  a Alan's score is 64.
     What is Jamal's score?   [1 mark]
  b Jamal takes his turn and goes into the lead.
     How many points could Jamal have scored on his turn?   [2 marks]

Callum invents a game.
Players can score either 2 points or 4 points on one play.

  c **i** Show how a player's **total** score could be 14 points.   [1 mark]
     ii Which numbers will the pointers on the board never point at?   [2 marks]

2 **a** In a car park, 1 car in every 4 is silver.
     There are 88 cars in the car park.
     How many silver cars are in the car park?   [1 mark]
  b Mother and Child spaces account for 3 out of every 25 spaces. There are 12 Mother and Child spaces in the car park.
     How many parking spaces are in the car park?   [2 marks]

3 Solve these equations.
  a $4x = 10$ [1 mark]

  b $3x - 5 = 43$ [2 marks]

  c $12 = 5 + \dfrac{x}{5}$ [2 marks]

4 This is a drawing of the Apollo 5 rocket that was used to launch moon missions.

It was built in three stages with the Moon Lander on top.

a The mass of the rocket, fully loaded with fuel, was eight thousand two hundred and twenty tonnes.

Write this number using figures. [1 mark]

b The first stage of the rocket was 42.07 metres high.
Write this number correct to 1 decimal place. [1 mark]

c Here is some information about the length of the rocket's three stages.

Total length including Moon Lander	110.65 m
Stage 1 length	42.07 m
Stage 2 length	24.84 m
Stage 3 length	17.87 m

How long is the Moon Lander? [2 marks]

d Apollo used 18 488 kg of rocket fuel.
Change 18 488 kg into tonnes. [1 mark]

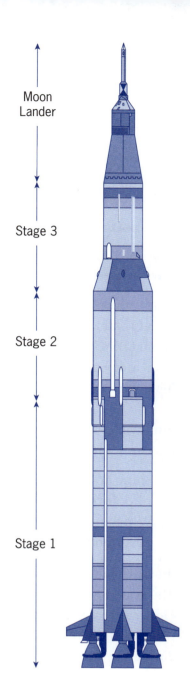

5 Helen's football team plays in League 1. These are the League 1 results one day in the 2009 – 2010 season. A score of 2–1 means that the home team scored two goals and the away team scored 1 goal.

Home team	Score	Away team
Brentford	1 - 1	Charlton
Colchester	2 - 1	Southampton
Exeter	1 - 1	Gillingham
Huddersfield	1 - 0	MK Dons
Leyton Orient	1 - 2	Southend
Millwall	2 - 0	Bristol Rovers
Stockport	2 - 4	Leeds United
Swindon	3 - 1	Yeovil
Tranmere	0 - 0	Carlisle
Wycombe	2 - 5	Brighton

Helen plans to tally the numbers of goals **each team** scored and draw a chart of her results.

a Which team scored 5 goals? [1 mark]

b Copy and complete this tally chart Helen has drawn. [3 marks]

Number of goals	Tally	Frequency
0	||||	4
1		
2		
3		
4		
5		

c Draw a bar chart showing your results. [3 marks]

d Helen says: The average number of goals scored by a team on this day is less than 2.

Damon says: Your average is different to mine!

When they check their working neither Helen nor Damon has made a mistake. Explain what has happened. [4 marks]

6 Three points **A**, **B** and **C** are plotted on the grid below.

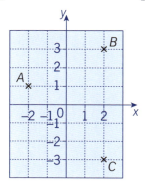

    a Write down the coordinates of point **A**. [1 mark]

    b **P** is the midpoint of the line **BC**.
Copy the grid and plot the point **P** (2, 0). [1 mark]

    c Join **A** to **B** and measure **AB**. Write down the length in centimetres. [1 mark]

    d Mark the midpoint of **AB** and write down its coordinates. [2 marks]

7 **a** Write down the next two terms in each sequence.
    i 4, 6, 9, 13, ..., ... [1 mark]
    ii 440, 220, 110, ..., ... [1 mark]

  b Write down the term-to-term rule for this sequence.
    12, 15, 18, 21, ... [1 mark]

  c Another sequence has the nth term
$$3n - 4$$
    i Write down the first, fifth and tenth terms of this sequence. [2 marks]
    ii Write down a term in the sequence that is between 440 and 450. [2 marks]

8 The table shows the numbers of minutes that flights from a small airport were delayed in one day. No flights were delayed more than 100 minutes.

Number of minutes delay	Number of flights
0 to 20	5
21 to 40	6
41 to 60	2
61 to 80	3
81 to 100	4

Calculate an estimate of the mean number of minutes that a flight had been delayed. [4 marks]

Practice paper A

9 Corrine is going on holiday to America.
She is allowed one bag weighing 32 kg on the plane.
Corrine's scales show weight in pounds and stones.
Corrine weighs her bag.

14 pounds = 1 stone

2.2 pounds = 1 kilogram

Will Corrine be allowed to take the bag on the plane?
You must show your working. [4 marks]

10 a The sketch shows a trapezium, made by joining three
equilateral triangles. One sloping edge is 6 cm long.

Not to scale

Use ruler and compasses only to construct the
trapezium accurately. [3 marks]

b This is a parallelogram, **ABCD**.
Use ruler and compasses only and construct the region
that is:
- Closer to **A** than **C** and,
- Closer to **AB** than **BC**.

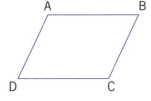

[3 marks]

11 Karen has these metal strips. She needs to join three of them
to make a right-angled triangle to support a structure she is making.

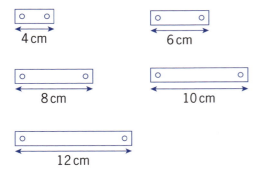

Show how Karen can do this. [4 marks]

Practice paper A

Unit B Foundation Practice Paper

60 marks   **1 hour**   **No calculator**

1 Work out
   - a $43 + 107 + 79$ [1 mark]
   - b $4.3 + 10.7 + 0.79$ [1 mark]
   - c 34×6 [1 mark]
   - d 3.4×0.6 [1 mark]

2 This rectangle has sides with length $3a + 5$ and width $2a$.

   a Write an expression for the total distance around the rectangle.
   Give your answer in the simplest possible form.   [2 marks]

   b a is a whole number and $a > 5$.
   - i Copy and complete the following statement about the rectangle.

     Length > _____.   [1 mark]

   - ii Show the possible values for the **width** on a copy of this number line.

     [2 marks]

Don't forget the scale.

3 a Copy and complete the labels for the parts of this circle.

   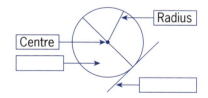

   [2 marks]

   b The diagram is accurate and drawn using four straight lines. Use the diagram to help you copy and complete the table with two words in each case. The first one has been done for you.

   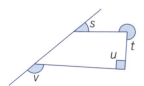

Angle s is	an acute	angle
Angle t is		angle
Angle u is		angle
Angle v is		angle

   [3 marks]

4 Work out
  i $\sqrt{64} + 3$ [1 mark]
  ii 25 [1 mark]
  iii 25 − 32 [1 mark]
 b Find the value of p in the following.
  i $33 \times 34 = 3^p$ [1 mark]
  ii $\dfrac{5^2 \times 5^3}{5^5} = p$

  Write your answer in the simplest possible form. [2 marks]

5 This question is about these quadrilaterals

| Rhombus | Square | Rectangle |
| Trapezium | Parallelogram | Kite |

 a What is the mathematical name of this shape?

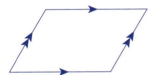

[1 mark]

 b Kelly has some clue cards.
  Each one gives a new clue to a quadrilateral.
  Each clue knocks out one or more quadrilaterals.
  For each clue write down the name of the quadrilateral(s) knocked out until one quadrilateral is left.
  i My angles are not right angles. [1 mark]
  ii My sides are not all equal. [1 mark]
  iii None of my sides are parallel. [1 mark]
  iv I am a _____ [1 mark]

6 Hexagon **B** is an enlargement of hexagon **A**.

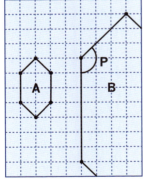

 a What is the scale factor of the enlargement? [1 mark]
 b The angle marked p is 135°. [2 marks]
  Give reasons for how you know this is true.
  (No marks will be given for measuring the angle.)
 c Copy and complete hexagon **B**. [2 marks]

Practice paper B

7 Sort all of these numbers into two groups.
One group is 'recurring decimals'.
Explain your second group and show any working you use.

| $\frac{2}{3}$ | | $\frac{1}{20}$ | | $\frac{3}{9}$ | | 0.2222 | | $\frac{2}{5}$ |

| 0.15 | | $\frac{40}{100}$ |

[4 marks]

8 Khalid is going on holiday in his car.
He has this information.

Number of miles travelled on one gallon of fuel	43.8
Length of journey (in miles)	2130
Number of litres in one gallon	4.5
Cost of one litre of fuel in pence	111.9

Calculate an estimate of the cost of the fuel Khalid will use.

[4 marks]

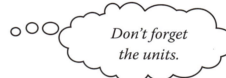

Don't forget the units.

9 Carrie has a game of 'Fraction Bingo'
The board is marked with fractions. She has counters marked as percentages.
Carrie puts one counter on a square so that the percentage matches the value of the fraction.
She does this until she cannot match any more percentages and fractions.

Carrie's counters

Carrie's board

	$\frac{1}{2}$	$\frac{1}{4}$	$\frac{3}{5}$
$\frac{3}{4}$			$\frac{1}{10}$
$\frac{3}{10}$	$\frac{3}{2}$	$\frac{3}{8}$	

Which counters can Carrie put on her board and which fractions will remain uncovered? You must show your working.

[4 marks]

Practice paper B

10 a Brian has kept this record of the number of units of electricity he used in each **quarter** (three months) for the last three years.

2007	Number of units	2008	Number of units	2009	Number of units	2010	Number of units
Spring	2400	Spring	2100	Spring	2000	Spring	1800
Summer	1800	Summer	1800	Summer	1500	Summer	1400
Autumn	2100	Autumn	2000	Autumn	1800	Autumn	
Winter	2800	Winter	2600	Winter	2400	Winter	

  i Copy and complete this time series graph.
  The first ten figures have been plotted for you.

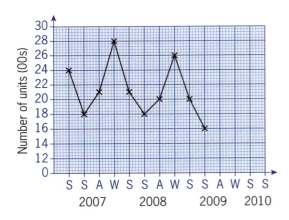

[2 marks]

  ii Draw a trend line on your graph. [1 mark]
  iii Use the graph to estimate the number of units
  Brian might use in the Autumn quarter of 2010 [2 marks]

b Brian asks two electricity companies. Prolec and Ecost, for information about their prices. He draws this graph showing how much electricity from the two companies will cost as he uses more units.
Brain will pay for the electricity he uses each month.

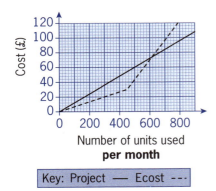

Key: Project —— Ecost ---

Use information from the graphs to recommend a company for Brian to use. [5 marks]

Practice paper B

11 The diagram shows a triangle with one line extended.
Copy and complete the proof that the exterior angle is equal to the sum of the two interior opposite angles.

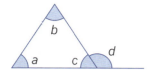

$a + b + c = 180°$ because angles in a triangle add up to 180°
$a + b = 180°$ .... [1 mark]
$c + d = 180°$ because .... [1 mark]

$d = 180° - c$
This shows that $d = 180° - c = $ .... [1 mark]

12 Barry has a one year old Skogo car.
He is planning to sell it and wants an estimate of its value.
He finds these ages of some Skogo cars and their sale values.

Age (years)	5	4	3	2	7	2	4	6	3	4.5
Value (£ 000)	5	5.0	5.8	6.7	3.1	5.7	4.2	3.6	5.2	4.6

Estimate the value of Barry's car.

Show your working.
You may wish to plot a graph. [5 marks]

Unit C Foundation Practice Paper

100 marks   **1½ hours**

1   Cally buys this soup mix to serve at the club.
    Usually 40 to 50 people turn up.
    She needs 17g of soup mix to serve one person. How much does she spend on soup so that she is sure to have enough for everyone?

    [4 mark]

2   This clock shows the time Amy arrives at Abbeyshaw station.
    a   What is the time shown on the clock?

    [1 mark]

b   This timetable shows her train to Down Heath, where she will get off the train and walk to her friend's house.

Abbeyshaw	Arrive	10:25
	Depart	10:27
Down Heath	Arrive	10:50
	Depart	10:52

The walk will take her 6 minutes.
How many minutes after she arrived at **Abbeyshaw station** will Amy reach her friend's house?   [3 marks]

3   Barry says,

> If people are asked to say a number between 0 and 10 then these numbers are not random.

Jenny asks some of her friends to say a number between 0 and 10.
These are her results.

    1   0   2   2   4   0   9   2   3   2
    5   2   7   3   9   10 2   1   1   1

a   What is the probability that the number 1 was said?   [2 marks]

b   Do Jenny's results suggest Barry is right or wrong?
    You must give reasons.   [3 marks]

c Barry did a similar survey.
These are his results.

Number	0	1	2	3	4	5	6	7	8	9	10
Number of people who said the number	20	35	40	20	50	65	24	70	35	20	21

Whose survey is more reliable?
You must give a reason for your choice. [1 mark]

d Karen did her survey.
She found that the probability of saying a number from 0 to 9 was 0.85.
What was the probability of saying 10 in Karen's survey? [1 mark]

4 Calculate

a $\dfrac{2}{5}$ of £17.20 [2 marks]

b $3\dfrac{1}{3} \div 5$ [1 mark]

5 Karl glues one centimetre glass tiles onto the edges of square mirrors to make a decorative border, like this.
  a How many tiles will Karl use to make a border around a mirror that has edge 10 cm long?
  [3 marks]

  b Karl has 20 mirrors, all with sides of 10 cm.
  Coloured tiles are sold in packets of 50.
  Each packet costs £2.70.

  How much will Karl pay to buy enough tiles for all the mirrors? [4 marks]

6 a Calculate the area of this rectangle with height 5.2 cm and length 12.4 cm. [2 marks]

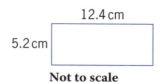

Not to scale

  b An isosceles triangle with the same height as the rectangle in **part (a)** is joined to the rectangle.

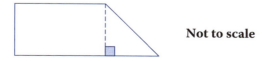

Not to scale

Calculate the area of the trapezium. [2 marks]

Practice paper C

7 This is Linda's Special Offer Menu in her café

Starter	**Main**	**Dessert**
Soup	Roast of the day	Trifle
Mushroom bruschetta	Vegetable risotto	Almond pastry
	Fish and chips	Cheese board
	Gammon and chips	

Any 2-course meal £7
Choose:
• Starter and Main or
• Main and Dessert or
• Starter and Dessert

a Copy and complete this table to show the choices Ian could make if he chose a Starter and Main.

	Roast of the day (R)	Vegetable risotto (V)	Fish and chips (F)	Gammon and chips (G)
Soup (S)	SR			
Mushroom bruschetta (M)				MG

[3 marks]

b What is the probability that Ian chose fish and chips, if he liked all the meals equally? [2 marks]

c How many different, **two** course, choices could be made from Linda's Special Offer menu? [4 marks]

8 A cereal company prints masks on **one face** of a cereal packet. Children cut these out and colour them.

They decide to print a mask on a larger box.
They use a scale factor 2 for the sides of the box and the mask.

Explain whether these statements are true or false.

Not to scale

a Each mask will be twice as wide and twice as high as the smaller mask. [1 mark]

b The bigger box will contain twice the weight of cereal as the smaller box. [3 marks]

Practice paper C

9 The graph represents Amy's sponsored walk.
The walk was on some flat ground and over some hills.
A road was crossed twice and there was a lunch break.
Amy finished the walk at the place where she started.

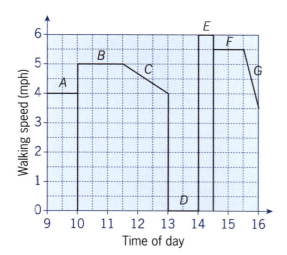

- **a** Write down the time when Amy first crossed the road. [1 mark]

- **b** On which section was Amy going uphill?
  Give a reason for your choice. [1 mark]

- **c** What was Amy's slowest walking speed? [1 mark]

- **d** How far did Amy walk in section E? [2 marks]

10 a Simplify
   - **i** $5a + a + 3a$ [1 mark]
   - **ii** $3k + 2m - 2k + m$ [2 marks]

   b Multiply out and simplify
   $3(2d + 3) - 5$ [2 marks]

   c Factorise
   $14x^2 + 7x$ [2 marks]

11 **a** Alex goes to the sales.

She likes this dress but the price tag has fallen off.
Its **full price** is £75.

What is the price of the dress in the sale? [3 marks]

b Alan sees this headline in a paper.

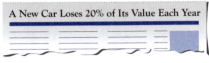

Wow, a car will be worth nothing after five years!

Alan says...

  i Show that the value of a car costing £10 000 when new is £6400 after two years. [3 marks]

  ii Show that Alan is wrong. [4 marks]

12 Jean has £12 000 to invest for one year.
She sees these two accounts.

ONE-YEAR BOND	HALF-YEAR ACCOUNT
4% interest paid on the account at the end of the year.	2% interest added to the account after 6 months. 2% paid on all savings at the end of the year.

The company claims that the half-year account
pays much more interest than the one-year bond.

Is this claim justified? [5 marks]

13 Use your calculator to work these out.

a $\sqrt{3.7^2 + 2.31}$ [2 marks]

b $\dfrac{1.2 + 4.3^2}{5.6^2 - 10.36}$ [3 marks]

Write your answer to 2 significant figures.

14 Clive's garden is a rectangle. He is going to make the whole garden into a lawn.

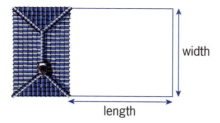

He measures the length = 40 m and the width = 18 m both **correct to the nearest metre.**

   a   What is the smallest possible length the garden
       could be? [1 mark]

   b   Clive needs 40g of grass seed for each square metre
       of lawn.
       How many square metres of lawn will one 5 kg bag of
       seed cover? [2 marks]

   c   Explain why measuring the length and width of his
       garden to the nearest metre will not affect the price
       Clive pays to have enough seed for his lawn.
                                                    [5 marks]

15 a Copy and complete the table of values for $y = \frac{1}{2}x + 2$

x	−4	0	4
y		2	

   [1 mark]

b Using graph paper, draw the graph of $y = \frac{1}{2}x + 2$ for values of x from −4 to 4.

[2 marks]

c Copy and complete the table of values for $y = 6 - x^2$.

x	−3	−2	−1	0	1	2	3
y	−3	2		6	5		−3

[1 mark]

d On the **same** grid, draw the graph of $y = 6 - x^2$ for values of x from −3 to 3. [2 marks]

e State the coordinates of the points where the graphs cross. [2 marks]

f Use your results to solve the equation

$6 - x^2 = \frac{1}{2}x + 2.$ [1 mark]

16 Lisa makes this open box from a sheet of squared paper (each small square is 1 cm²).

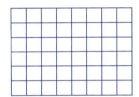 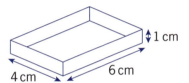

a Show how the net may be made by cutting just four squares from the sheet of paper. [1 mark]

b Work out the surface area of the **outside** of the open box. [2 marks]

c Work out the volume of the open box. [2 marks]

d Graham said, "Any open box you make from that piece of paper will have the same surface area and volume." Show whether Graham is right or wrong. [4 marks]

Answers

Unit A

Ex AN1

1. **a** −2 **b** 128 **c** −29 **d** −13
2. **a**

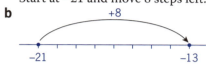

Start at −21 and move 8 steps left.

b

Start at −21 and move 8 steps right.

3. **a** + × − is − **b** + ÷ − is −
   c − × − × − = + × − = − **d** + × − = −
4. 192
5. 19°C
6. **a** 89p **b** 90p
7. **a** 330 mm **b** 47.1 mm **c** 25.7 mm
   d The height growth rate of boys is almost double that of girls between 11 and 18. However, girls start their growth in puberty earlier than 11 as shown by the fact that they are taller than boys on average at the beginning of the time period analysed
8. −5, −3, −2
9. **a** 2160 inches **b** 180 ft

Ex AN2

1. **a** 0.002 **b** 23 483 920 000 **c** 34 800
2. **a** 63 360 inches **b** 4576 yards **c** 1956
3. **a** it must be smaller than 123
   b it must be more than 16
   c the answer cannot have more than 1 decimal place
   d the digits have not moved at all
   e it must be bigger than 1.4
   f the digits multiply to give 5 not 6
   g the decimal point must move 2 places to the left
4. $12\tfrac{1}{2}$ pence
5. **a** 4200 mm **b** 1060 m
   c yes – the bracket is 100 mm wide which is more than half the width of the shelf
   d No – the drive would need to be 163.4 m long
6. 9091 km

Ex AN3

1. **a** eleven thousand, three hundred and eighty-four
   b two million, ten thousand, three hundred and forty-five
   c four million, five hundred thousand and twenty
   d twenty three million, four hundred and forty four thousand and twelve
2. **a** 12609 **b** 50 120 007
   c 142.2 **d** 15 905 053
3. **a** 12.3<u>7</u>6 **b** 0.00<u>4</u>69
   c 25.09<u>3</u>6 **d** <u>3</u>.5398
4. **a** 12.38 **b** 0.0 **c** 25.094 **d** 3.54
5. **a** 1<u>2</u>.376 **b** 0.00<u>4</u>69
   c <u>2</u>5.0936 **d** <u>3</u>.5398
6. **a** 140 300 **b** 30 000 **c** 0.6 **d** 17.1
   e 50 000 **f** 1.97 **g** 3 **h** 0.003
   i 825.77 **j** 17.0
7. **a** 1.7 **b** 21 **c** 0.14 **d** 7.7
8. £19.18
9. **a** £28.38 **b** 231 **c** 12p
   d 20p **e** £17.82

Ex AN4

1. **a** 6, 12, 18, 24, 30 **b** 8, 16, 24, 32, 40
   c 17, 34, 51, 68, 85 **d** 23, 46, 69, 92, 115
   e 51, 102, 153, 204, 255
   f 242, 484, 726, 968, 1210
2. **a** 1, 2, 4, 8, 16 **b** 1, 3, 7, 21
   c 1, 2, 3, 4, 6, 9, 12, 18, 36 **d** 1, 43
   e 1, 2, 3, 4, 5, 6, 8, 10, 12, 15, 20, 24, 30, 40, 60, 120
   f 1, 2, 3, 4, 6, 8, 12, 23, 24, 46, 69, 92, 138, 184, 276, 552
3. 31, 37, 41, 43, 47
4. **a** no **b** yes **c** no
   d no **e** no **f** yes
5. **a** $2 \times 3 \times 5$ **b** $2^3 \times 3^2$ **c** 2×7^2
   d $2 \times 5 \times 13$ **e** 2×83 **f** 2^{10}
6. **a** 60 **b** 48 **c** 132 **d** 60 **e** 180
7. **a** 6 **b** 8 **c** 2 **d** 1 **e** 3
8. 10 o'clock

Ex AN5

1. **a** 6.25 **b** 25 **c** 0.784
   d 11 **e** 3 **f** 4.79
   g 3.3 **h** 0.1 **i** −154.7
2. **a** 0.2 **b** 5 **c** 0.08$\dot{3}$ **d** 0.01 **e** 0.0$\dot{5}$ **f** 12.8
   a and **b** are reciprocals of one another
3. **a** £2.60 **b** £25.98
4. **a** 22.4 km **b** 20 miles
5. 1044 grams
6. £4600

Ex AN6

1. **a** 19.5 **b** 2.9 **c** 9.8
   d −5.2 **e** −0.8 **f** 36.4
2. **b** $4 - 3 \div 2 = 4 - 1.5 = 2.5$
   c $(1 + 4) \times 3 - 6 = 15 - 6 = 9$
   d $4 - 2 \times (3 + 1) = 4 - 8 = -4$
   e $3 - (2 \times 1.5 + 1) = 3 - 4 = -1$
   f $12 + 2(3 \times 4) - 2 = 12 + 24 - 2 = 34$
3. **a** 5 **b** 5.8 **c** 9.25 **d** 0.7
   e 9 **f** 4.1 **g** 4.2 **h** 49
4. **a** $(1 + 2) \times 3 = 9$ **b** $1 + 2 \times (3 - 4) = -1$
   c $10 - (3 + 2) \times 5 = -15$
   d $(10 - 3 + 2) \times 5 = 45$
   e $10 - (3 + 2 \times 5) = -3$
   f $(14 + 5) \times 2^2 = 76$
   g $14 + (5 \times 2)^2 = 114$
   h $12 - (2 + 5 \times 2) + 1 = 1$
5. **a** 3 **b** $\dfrac{(12 + 3) \times 2}{10}$

6 **a** No   **b** £25 + £15 × 3   **c** £70

Ex AN7

1 **a** 2:3   **b** 4:3   **c** 2:3   **d** 3:1
   e 2:3:4   **f** 5:2:6   **g** 4:1:3   **h** 3:4
   i 24:3:8   **j** 10:1
2 **a** 1:4   **b** 1:0.5   **c** 1:1.5
   d 1:2.5   **e** 1:0.2   **f** 1:0.22
3 **a** 1.25:1   **b** 0.4:1   **c** 1.25:1
   d $1\frac{2}{3}$:1   **e** 6:1   **f** 0.875:1
4 **a** 5:12   **b** 1:300   **c** 1:5
   d 20:1   **e** 1:7   **f** 1:48
5 **a** 8:3:6   **b** 8:12:1   **c** 1:2:10
   d 2:1:50   **e** 480:1:110   **f** 30:2:9
6 **a** $\frac{2}{5}$ **b** $\frac{1}{2}$ **c** $\frac{5}{9}$
   d $\frac{1}{2}$ **e** $\frac{2}{5}$ **f** $\frac{4}{15}$

Ex AN8

1 **a** £5:£20   **b** 140 g:60 g   **c** 1.05 kg:1.75 kg
   d 100 mins:60 mins:20 mins
2 **a** 8.1 kg   **b** £10.25   **c** 72p
   d W = 0.5 litres, X = 7.5 litres
3 **a i** £60.75   **ii** £109.35   **b** £1458
4 **a** 36 m²   **b** $\frac{2}{9}$
5 **a** 2.5 g   **b** 35:6   **c** 2:3
   d there is $1\frac{1}{2}$ times as much fibre as fat
   e Fat equals 0.096 of the biscuit which is less than 0.1 or $\frac{1}{10}$. Therefore TRUE.
6 **a** 630 miles   **b** Yes – he claims £336
7 **a** Hint 25:3
   b 1.875 litres of red and 1.125 litres of white
   c Pale   **d** 5.6 litres

Ex AA1

1 **a** $8a + 7a = 15a$ **b** $6b + 5b = 11b$
   c $3c + 5c = 8c$ **d** $8c + 13b = 21c$
   e $9t + 23t = 32t$ **f** $18b + 8b = 26b$
   g $13c - 8c = 5c$ **h** $6c - 6c = 0$
   i $15s - 7s = 8s$ **j** $13b - 6b = 7b$
2 **a** $3m$ **b** $7n$ **c** $6y$ **d** $3z$
3 **a** $13a$ **b** $17n$ **c** $15t$ **d** $19x$
   e $4r$ **f** $4f$ **g** $7g$ **h** $8r$
   i $23n$ **j** $17c$
4 **a** $4m$ **b** $3p$ **c** rs **d** $12q$
   e $5g$ **f** $4c$ **g** $8d$ **h** jk
   i n^2 **j** $15e$ **k** t^2 **l** $6mn$
5 **a** $15n$ **b** $12m$ **c** $17p$ **d** $18q$
   e x **f** $4w$ **g** $7a$ **h** $5b$
   i j **j** $2k$
6 **a** $\frac{d}{4}$ **b** $\frac{x}{3}$ **c** $\frac{y}{7}$ **d** $\frac{t}{9}$
   e $\frac{2a}{3}$ **f** $\frac{3n}{4}$ **g** $\frac{5p}{7}$ **h** $\frac{v}{2}$
7 **a** $3x + 5x + 7x - 2x$ **b** $3x + 5x + 2x - 7x$
   c $7x + 3x + 2x - 5x$ **d** $7x + 5x + 2x - 3x$

8 **a** $3b$ **b** $11v$ **c** $4y$ **d** c^4
   e $9s + 13t$ **f** $4j + 7k$ **g** $4z^3$
   h $-g - 9h$ **i** 0
9 **a** equation   **b** expression   **c** formula
   d formula   **e** equation   **f** expression

Ex AA2

1 A(4, 4)   B(0, 2)   C(5, 0)   D(−5, 1)
   E(−3, 0)   F(-4, −1)   G(0, −3)   H(1, −1)
2 **a**

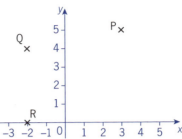

   b (3, −1); (8, 2). Other answers are possible – either need PS parallel to QR or RS parallel to QP.
3 (5, −7)   {or (−3, −7)}
4 **i a** (2.5, 3)   **b** (4, 2)   **c** (2.5, −1)
   d (−1, −2)   **e** (−1, 5.5)   **f** (3.5, −1)
   ii a 5   **b** 7.21   **c** 9.22
   d 6.32   **e** 17   **f** 7.28
5 **a** (5, −4)
   b M(0, 1), N(4, 3)
   Length MN = $\sqrt{4^2 + 2^2} = \sqrt{20}$

Ex AA3

1 £248.37
2 **a** 15   **b** 57   **c** 18
   d 9   **e** −9   **f** 1
3 **a** $C = £(pw + 4)$ **b** $A = \frac{1}{2}\pi r^2 - 3vh$
4 **a** $x = \frac{y}{a}$ **b** $x = m + t$ **c** $x = pr$
   d $x = k - z$ **e** $x = \frac{a+7}{5}$ **f** $x = \frac{y-c}{m}$
   g $x = \frac{t+9}{w}$ **h** $x = \frac{s-ab}{r}$ **i** $x = \frac{q}{r} + z$
   j $x = 3m - f$ **k** $x = \frac{y}{p}$ **l** $x = t(c + d)$
5 **a** $a = \frac{A}{\pi b}$ **b** 94.2 cm²
   A stamping machine has to leave gaps between the ellipses

Ex AA4

1 **a** 23, 26   Add 3 each time
   b 48, 96   Double each time
   c 9, 3   Subtract 6 each time
   d 3, 1   Divide by 3 each time
   e 6, −2   Subtract 8 each time
   f $4\frac{1}{2}, 2\frac{1}{4}$ Divide by 2 each time
2 **a** 16, 21   **b** 8, 15   **c** 10, 20   **d** 1.6, 1.8
   e 10, 8   **f** 20, 0   **g** 2, 6   **h** −1, 4
3 **a** 87   **b** 0
4 **a** Pattern

b

Pattern	1	2	3	4
No of squares	3	5	7	9

    c 201

5 $5n + 1$

6 a Because the length of the spring goes up by the same amount each time

    b $3.5n + 34.5$ cm   c 19

Ex AA5

1 a 4   b 19   c 60   d 7   e 3.5
    f −4   g 7   h 80   i −1   j 5
    k 3.5   l 4   m 75   n 8   o −5
    p 5   q 4   r 3.5   s 3   t −4
    u −3   v 6   w −2   x −19

2 a £16   b $2h + 10 = 38$; 14 hours

3 a $x = 12$; angles are 60°, 120°, 60°, 120°
    b parallelogram

4 $3x + 4x − 20 + x + 40 = 180$; $x = 20$
    a 60°, 60°, 60°   b equilateral

5 a $4x + 3 = 19$ and $7x + 15 = 43$ so not correct
    b $4x − 7x = −3x$ not $3x$ c −4

Ex AA6

1 a $4c + 20$ b $7y + 49$ c $p^2 − 7p$
    d $y^2 + yz$ e $2e^2 + 10ef$ f $9f^2 + 12hf$

2 a $5(h − 4)$ b $7(4 + k)$ c $f(f + 9)$
    d $4(y + 3)$ e $6(3d − 4)$ f $20(2 − 3m)$
    g $q(p − q)$ h $3g(g + 2)$ i $4n(2m + 3n)$

3 $2mn − 8m$

4 a 3   b 5   c −2.5   d 3
    e 6   f 28   g $-\frac{1}{2}$

5 a i $x + 10$ ii $2x + 20$
    b $4x + 30 = 182$; 38

6 a $10(x − 4) + 2(3x + 5) + 5(20 − x) = 180$; $x = 10$
    b 60°, 70°, 50°   c Acute angled or scalene

Ex AG1

1 a 2.75 kg   b 78.5°
2 a gm   b m   c cm   d kg   e litres
3 a gallons   b stones   c miles
4 a 3000 g   b 48 pints   c 1 stone 5 lbs
    d 3.5 cm   e 42 inches   f 8 ft 6 inches
    g 400 cm   h 38.5 lbs   i 0.6 litres
    j $1\frac{1}{2}$ ft
5 a 120 cm   b $7\frac{1}{2}$ kg
    c 18 litres   d 6 litres
6 a $6\frac{2}{3}$ ft   b 15.6 miles
    c 26.4 lbs   d 28 pints
7 253 km
8 6360 (3 sf)

Ex AG2

1 Standard constructions
2 Standard constructions

3 36.9°, 53.1°, 90°. Right angled
4 6.1 cm
5 72°
6 Standard construction
7 Standard constructions
8 Construct arcs centre A radius 10 cm and centre B radius 10 cm. Join the point of intersection of these arcs to A to form a line at 60° to AB. Now construct a perpendicular from B onto this line using a standard construction. Where the perpendicular meets the line gives the point P.
9 Standard construction

Ex AG3

1 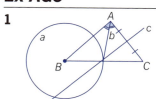

2 a Perpendicular bisector of XZ
    b Angle bisector of angle ZWX

3 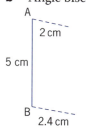

4 a 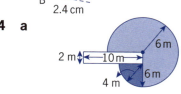

    b i 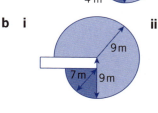   ii 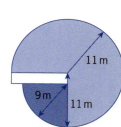

Ex AG4

1 $x = 150°$; $x = 325°$; $x = 55°$ $y = 80°$ $z = 3$ cm
2 13.8 km
3 Accurate scale drawing
4 £1.37

Ex AG5

1 a 250°   b 325°   c 110°
2 a West   b North East   c North West
3 a Accurate scale drawing
    b 020°
4 a Travel 9 km on a bearing of 035°, then 6 km on a bearing of 115°
    b 15 km. Direct distance = 11.7 km
5 a the peak of the third hill behind Six Hill
    b 125°

Ex AG6

1 $a = 4.2$ m $b = 9.1$ m $c = 12.2$ m $d = 18.3$ m

2 27.9 m
3 471.7 m
4 a 4   **b** 3   **c** 5
5 $x = 4$
6 a 13.7 m   **b** £11.90
7 No because $7^2 + 15^2 \neq 17^2$

Ex AS1

1

		Shoe sizes				
		3	4	5	6	7	8
Glove sizes	XS					
	Small		9			
	Medium				7	
	large					

2

	Red	Blue	Green	Black	Silver	Other
Car						
Lorry						
Bus or coach						
Van						
Other						

3 a

		Across answers				
	Word length	4	5	6	7	8	9
Down answers	5					
	6				12	
	7					
	8					
	9					
	10					

b She only asked her work colleagues so
  1 excluded certain age groups (e.g. those at school)
  2 excluded people who do other types of work

4 a does not include all hair colours e.g. red; does not distinguish between natural hair colour and dyed hair colours.
Should ask "What colour is your hair at the moment?"
Blonde   Brown   Black   Red   Other
b OK
c This is subjective – need to have some accurate way of describing short, medium and long hair for both men and women
d Need 2 extra categories: Less than once a week
More than twice but not every day
e Would be better to ask "How often do you use conditioner?"
Always   Sometimes   Never

Ex AS2

1 a 20   **b** 14
  c i bimodal 12 and 16   **ii** 14   **iii** 13.7
  d i there is no single mode   **ii** 14.5   **iii** 14
2 For multiplication test, mode = 20, median = 19 and mean = 17.7
For division test, mode = 19, median = 17 and mean = 17
This suggests that the students were slightly better at multiplication than division (although there is more variation in the multiplication test results as seen by a range of 16 compared to a range of 10 for the division tests)

3 a 24.3 mins
b

0	9
1	1 5 6
2	0 2 3 4 8 9
3	0 1 2 4
4	1

Key 2|3 means 23 minutes

Ex AS3

1 a i 9   **ii** 9   **b** 8.8
2 a £35.38   **b** £30.38
3 The mode as that is an actual size (7) and is the most frequent sale. Note that the median is also 7, but the mean is approx 6.98 which is not an actual shoe size.
4 a 68.6 mins   **b** $60 < m \leqslant 80$
  c there is not a prominent modal class. There are 3 very distinct peaks in the data with very similar frequencies
5 a May 3.8 hours   June 4.4 hours
  b i May $2 \leqslant h < 4$ June $4 \leqslant h < 6$
   ii May $2 \leqslant h < 4$ June $4 \leqslant h < 6$

Ex AS4

1

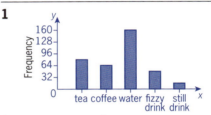

2 a 22   **b** $38 + 31 + 45 + 24 + 16 = 154$
  c Biology
3 a 28.8°   **b** 340
4 a 54   **b** $47 + 85 + 71 + 33 + 54 = 290$
  c Construct pie chart with angles: Bitton 58°, Fixttoll 106°, Gravely 88°, Holton 41°, and Sanvy 67°

Ex AS5

1 a

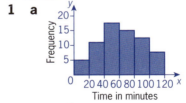

b

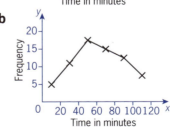

c $40 < m \leq 60$

2 a

Leaf length, l mm	Frequency
$20 < l \leq 30$	2
$30 < l \leq 40$	3
$40 < l \leq 50$	11
$50 < l \leq 60$	0
$60 < l \leq 70$	0
$70 < l \leq 80$	6
$80 < l \leq 90$	5
$90 < l \leq 100$	3

b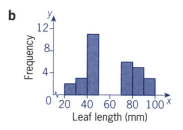

c Because there appears to be 2 different distributions, one with a modal class of $40 < l \leqslant 50$ and the other with a modal class of $70 < l \leqslant 80$.

3 a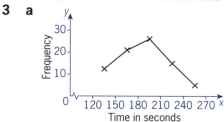

b The modal class for the swim to bike transition is 180 to 210 secs, whereas the modal class for the bike to run transition is 90 to 120 secs. On average, the swim to bike transition is roughly twice as long.

Unit B

Ex BN1

1. **a** 13.9 **b** 7.1 **c** 4.76 **d** 6.1 **e** 15.2 **f** 4.64 **g** 1.26 **h** 10.16 **i** 33.26
2. **a** 49.2 **b** 13.5 **c** 4.52 **d** 0.625 **e** 22 **f** 31.6 **g** 15.6 **h** 400 **i** 110 **j** 229 **k** 0.296 **l** 7.98
3. **a** 2.7 **b** 1.5 **c** 27 **d** 15 **e** 150
4. 14 miles
5. 21.7 mg
6. **a** 269.6 km **b** 98 km **c** 4.6 km
7. 5.7 cm
8. 46

Ex BN2

1. *a, c, d* are clearly wrong
2. **a** $12.6 + 2.7 = 15.3$ **b** $71 + 5 = 76$ **c** $0.25 \times 10 \div 2 = 2.5 \div 2 = 1.25$ **d** $4.1 \times 5 = 20.5$ **e** $(4 + 2) \div 6 = 1$ **f** $3 \times 1.5 - 2 = 4.5 - 2 = 2.5$
3. **a** $14 \div 2 = 7$ **b** $46 \times 11 = 506$ **c** $16 - 4 = 12$ **d** $(106 + 5) \div 11 = 111 \div 11 \approx 10$ **e** $6 \times 4 = 24$ **f** $12^2 - 14 = 144 - 14 = 130$
4. **a** $\frac{14+8}{15-10}$ **b** $22 \div 5 = 44 \div 10 = 4.4$
5. Estimated cost of units = £0.25 × 100 = £25

   VAT at 5% = £25 × $\frac{5}{100}$ = £$\frac{125}{100}$ = £1.25

   Estimated bill ≈ £26

Ex BN3

1. **a** $\frac{3}{10}$ **b** $\frac{3}{100}$ **c** $1\frac{27}{100}$ **d** $11\frac{9}{100}$ **e** $6\frac{101}{1000}$

2. **a** $\frac{2}{5}$ **b** $\frac{1}{20}$ **c** $1\frac{1}{4}$ **d** $11\frac{14}{25}$ **e** $6\frac{1}{8}$ **f** $12\frac{11}{20}$ **g** $1\frac{81}{200}$ **h** $6\frac{127}{250}$ **i** $\frac{3}{200}$ **j** $21\frac{3}{500}$

3. **a** $T, \frac{111}{1000}$ **b** $R, 0.101101$ **c** $R, 0.502777$ **d** $T, 1\frac{1079}{5000}$

4. An exact price can only have two places after the decimal point to make whole cents. The nearest exact price is €9.67

5. **a** 24.9
   b No. His check is only an estimate and is roughly correct

Ex BN4

1. **a** 6, 16 **b** 18, 25, 90
2. **a** $\frac{1}{3}$ **b** $\frac{3}{5}$ **c** $\frac{1}{12}$ **d** $\frac{4}{7}$ **e** $\frac{1}{2}$ **f** $\frac{1}{4}$ **g** $\frac{4}{9}$ **h** $\frac{2}{3}$ **i** $\frac{2}{5}$ **j** $\frac{3}{10}$ **k** $\frac{2}{5}$ **l** $\frac{5}{12}$
3. **a** 97.8, 100.9, 102 **b** 0.219, 2.19, 21.9, 219 **c** 0.1, 0.18, 0.29, 0.3 **d** 6.04, 6.07, 6.17, 6.18 **e** 8.9, 9, 9.1, 9.11 **f** 3, 3.08, 3.79, 3.8
4. **a** $\frac{1}{4}, \frac{1}{2}, \frac{3}{4}$ **b** $\frac{5}{12}, \frac{2}{3}, \frac{5}{6}$ **c** $\frac{3}{10}, \frac{13}{20}, \frac{4}{5}$ **d** $\frac{1}{6}, \frac{7}{12}, \frac{3}{4}$ **e** $\frac{2}{3}, \frac{13}{18}, \frac{7}{9}$ **f** $\frac{1}{2}, \frac{3}{5}, \frac{13}{20}, \frac{7}{10}$
5. January
6. Second
7. **a** $A \frac{77}{200}$ $B \frac{23}{60}$ **b** B

Ex BN5

1. **a** £6 **b** 22.5 m **c** 10 km **d** 40 g **e** £7.20 **f** 16.8 km **g** £7.60 **h** 4.02 m
2. **a** $\frac{1}{20}$ **b** $\frac{7}{40}$ **c** $\frac{1}{31}$ **d** $\frac{1}{20}$
3. **a** $\frac{1}{2}$ **b** $\frac{1}{16}$ **c** 1 **d** $\frac{1}{4}$ **e** $\frac{7}{8}$ **f** $\frac{13}{15}$ **g** $3\frac{3}{5}$ **h** $\frac{5}{14}$ **i** $\frac{15}{44}$ **j** $2\frac{1}{2}$ **k** $2\frac{1}{2}$ **l** $\frac{4}{25}$
4. **a** 0.75 **b** 0.4 **c** 0.375 **d** 0.56 **e** 0.27 **f** 0.15
5. **a** $\frac{1}{8}$ **b** 1 **c** you always get 1
6. $\frac{2}{9}$
7. C
8. Statement 1 is correct in actual £ and pence because £3.42 × 7 = £23.94 (whereas £3.43 × 7 = £24.01 which exceeds the weekly amount). Statement 2 is *exact* because £$\frac{24}{7}$ = £$3\frac{3}{7}$

Ex BN6

1. **a** 0.35, 45%, $\frac{1}{2}$ **b** 0.07, 70%, $\frac{4}{5}$

    c 69%, $\frac{3}{4}$, 80%   **d** $\frac{2}{3}$, 68%, 0.7

2 0.52 (since $\frac{2}{5}$ = 0.4)

3 $\frac{28}{40}$ = 70% so Celine has the best score

4 0.35 (as this is $\frac{35}{100}$)

5 **a** 31.2 m   **b** 22 men   **c** £0.50   **d** £7.20
     e 9.6 g   **f** 78   **g** 28 km   **h** £462
     i 5.7 cm   **j** £55   **k** 5.4 m   **l** 420

6 Definitely not – correct answer is £87.40

7 Ian by £2.50

8 $\frac{7}{8} = \frac{4}{8} + \frac{2}{8} + \frac{1}{8} = \frac{1}{2} + \frac{1}{4} + \frac{1}{8}$
     = 50% + 25% + 12.5% = 87.5%

9

Fraction	Decimal	Percentage
$\frac{1}{100}$	0.01	1%
$\frac{7}{10}$	0.7	70%
$\frac{2}{5}$	0.4	40%

10 5%

Ex BN7

1 **a** 1   **b** 169   **c** 168
2 **a** 64   **b** 13   **c** 144   **d** 400
     e 13   **f** 0   **g** 133   **h** 10
     i 196   **j** 23
3 **a** 7   **b** 9   **c** 5   **d** 6
     e 11   **f** 12   **g** 3   **h** 2
4 **a** 20 cm   **b** 80 cm
5 120 cm

Ex BN8

1 **a** 2^6 **b** 3^3 **c** 5^5 **d** $2^2 \times 3^4$
     e $5^2 \times 6^4$ **f** $3^2 \times 10^3$
2 **a** $4 \times 4 \times 4$ **b** $5 \times 5 \times 5 \times 5$
     c $7 \times 7 \times 7 \times 7 \times 7 \times 7$ **d** $8 \times 8 \times 8 \times 8 \times 8$
     e $3 \times 3 \times 3 \times 2 \times 2 \times 2 \times 2 \times 2$
     f $4 \times 4 \times 4 \times 5 \times 5 \times 5$
     g $3 \times 3 \times 7 \times 7 \times 7 \times 7$
     h $9 \times 9 \times 9 \times 3 \times 3 \times 3 \times 3 \times 3 \times 3 \times 3 \times 3$
3 **a** 1000   **b** 16   **c** 1   **d** 200
     e 64   **f** 36   **g** 36   **h** 4
4 **a** 2^9 **b** 5^9 **c** 4^9 **d** 3^6
     e 6^2 **f** 5^2 **g** 10   **h** $4^5 \times 3^6$
     i $7^6 \times 4^3$ **j** $5^5 \times 3^3$ **k** $5^2 \times 4$ **l** $6^7 \times 5$
     m 2^5 **n** 4^2 **o** 7^2
5 2^8
6 No
7 **a** 2^{10} **b** 2, 4, 8, 16, 32, 64
     c **i** 6   **ii** 14   **iii** 30
     d It equals $2 \times$ [last number – 1]
        = 2 × (512 – 1) = 1022
        Alternatively find 2 + 4 + 8 + 16 + 32 + 64 + 128 + 256 + 512

Ex BA1

1

x	–2	2	5
y	1	5	8

2 Check graphs are straight lines through the following pairs of points:
     a (–4, –7) and (4, 1)   **b** (–4, –7) and (4, 9)
     c (–4, –13) and (4, 11)   **d** (–4, 14) and (4, 6)
     e (–4, 9) and (4, 1)   **f** (–4, 0) and (4, 4)
3 **a** $m = 6$ and $c = -2$ **b** $m = \frac{2}{3}$ and $c = 0$
     c $m = -1$ and $c = 8$
4 –3
5 **a** $x = 0.4, y = 4.8$ **b** $x = 3.5, y = 3.3$
     c $x = -0.3, y = 1.3$
6 $x = 1.1, y = 3.3$

Ex BA2

1 **a**

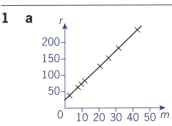

     b

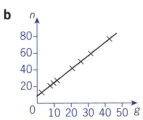

     c

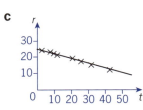

     d

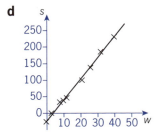

     e

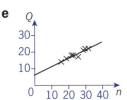

     f

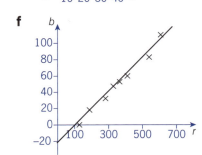

2
  a C = 15w + 30
  b Straight line graphs through the following points:
  Recipe book   (0, 20) and (6,140)
  Internet   (0, 30) and (6, 120)
  c w = 2 pounds
  d 20w + 20 = 15w + 30 so 5w = 10 and w = 2

3 **a** Cost £

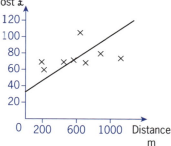

  b The scatter is so great that the line of best fit is not representative. Julia's idea is not a good one.

Ex BA3

1
  a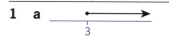
  b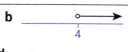
  c
  d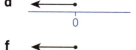
  e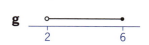
  f
  g
  h
  i

2
  a $x > 6$ **b** $x > 5$ **c** $x < 25$ **d** $y \leqslant 60$
  e $x \geqslant 3.5$ **f** $p \leqslant 4.5$ **g** $d > 18$ **h** $f < 15$
  i $r > 2\tfrac{1}{3}$ **j** $x \geqslant -1$ **k** $x < 1$ **l** $x \geqslant 10$
  m $v \leqslant \tfrac{1}{2}$ **n** $c > 1\tfrac{1}{2}$ **o** $r < -6$ **p** $-\tfrac{1}{2} < x < 5$
  q $-2 < x < 7$ **r** $7 \leqslant x \leqslant 11\tfrac{1}{2}$

3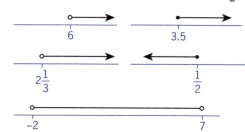

4 $3m + 7 \geqslant m + 25$ leading to $m \geqslant 9$
  9 is the smallest possible number in a packet

Ex BG1

1
  a $a = 42°$ $b = 78°$ $c = 36°$
  b $d = 108°$ $e = 58°$
  c $f = 65°$

2
  a $x = 71°$ (isosceles triangle)
  b $x = 40°$ (isosceles triangle)
  c $a = 64°$ (opposite angles)
     $b = 116°$ (angles at a point)
     $c = 64°$ (alternate angles)
     $d = 66°$ (angles at a point)
     $e = 50°$ (angles in a triangle)
     $f = 50°$ (opposite angles)

3 $a + b + c = 180°$ (angles at a point). But the other two unmarked angles of the triangle are b and a (alternate angles). Therefore the angles of the triangle add to 180°.

Ex BG2

1 **a** 101°   **b** 90°   **c** $a = 50°, b = 130°, c = 50°$
2 **a** 1080°   **b** $x = 50°$
3
  a Draw in a radius of the circle. Then using a protractor, draw a radius at intervals of 72°. This will give 5 points equally spaced on the circle. Join these 5 points.
  b Draw in a radius of the circle. Then using a protractor, draw a radius at intervals of 60°. This will give 6 points equally spaced on the circle. Join these 6 points.
  c Draw in a radius of the circle. Then using a protractor, draw a radius at intervals of $\dfrac{360}{n}$.
  This will give n points equally spaced on the circle. Join these n points.

4 140°, 40°

5
  a 3240° (can be divided into 18 triangles)
     162° (i.e. 3240 ÷ 20)
  b 20 × exterior angle = 360°, so exterior angle = 18°.
     Therefore, interior angle = 180° − 18° = 162°

6 Pentagons: No, because 360° is not divisible by the interior angle 108°
  Hexagons: Yes, because 360° is divisible by the interior angle 120° so three hexagons can be fitted together at a point and leave no gaps.

Ex BG3

1 **a** (7, 6)   **b** (6, 1)   **c** (1, 0)
       d (4, 4)   **e** (0, −2)

2 Check the image has vertices (−1, 2), (2, 3) and (1, 4)
$\begin{pmatrix} 1 \\ -3 \end{pmatrix}$

3 **a**    **b** $\begin{pmatrix} 4 \\ -1 \end{pmatrix}$

Ex BG4

1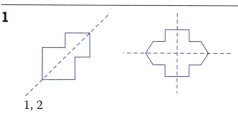

1, 2

2 Images will be triangles with vertices:
  a (2, 0), (0, −2), (3, −2)   **b** (2, 2), (3, 0), (0, 0)
  c (0, 2), (2, 3), (2, 0)

3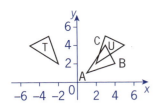

4

Regular polygon	Number of mirror lines	Order of rotational symmetry
Equilateral triangle	3	3
Square	4	4
Pentagon	5	5
Hexagon	6	6
Heptagon	7	7
Octagon	8	8

The order of rotational symmetry for a regular polygon is the same as the number of lines of reflection symmetry and equal to the number of sides.

5 a reflection in the line $y = 5$
b half-turn about (5, 4)
6 reflection in the line $x = 4$

Ex BG5

1 a $(-2, -3)$ **b i** $(-2, 2)$ **ii** $\begin{pmatrix} -5 \\ -1 \end{pmatrix}$

2 a Reflection in $y = 3$
Reflection in $x = 4\frac{1}{2}$
b Rotation of 90° about (0,0)
Reflection in $x = -3$

3 a Translation $\begin{pmatrix} 6 \\ 0 \end{pmatrix}$

b Translation $\begin{pmatrix} 0 \\ -6 \end{pmatrix}$

c Two successive reflections in 2 parallel lines is equivalent to a translation perpendicular to the lines through twice the distance between the lines

Ex BG6

1 a no, the right-hand triangle is a right-angled triangle but the left-hand triangle is not
b yes, angles in a triangle add up to 180°
c no, angles in a triangle add up to 180°
d yes, the left-hand triangle is three times the size of the right-hand triangle
2 a A and F; **b** B and D; **c** C and E;

Ex BG7

1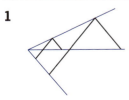

2 Images will be pentagons with the following vertices:
a $A_1(4, 2), B_1(8, 2), C_1(8, 4), D_1(6, 4)$ and $E_1(4, 6)$
b $A_2\left(4, 3\frac{1}{2}\right), B_2\left(5, 3\frac{1}{2}\right), C_2(5, 4),$
$D_2\left(4\frac{1}{2}, 4\right)$ and $E_2\left(4, 4\frac{1}{2}\right)$
c $A_3\left(2, 1\frac{1}{2}\right), B_3\left(3\frac{1}{2}, 1\frac{1}{2}\right), C_3\left(3\frac{1}{2}, 2\frac{1}{4}\right),$
$D_3\left(2\frac{3}{4}, 2\frac{1}{4}\right)$ and $E_3(2, 3)$

3 a Check graph
b Check vertices of image are as listed below
c $A_1(5, 2), B_1(7, 4), C_1(9, 0), D_1(6, 0)$
4 a yes – this is an enlargement SF 2
b yes – this is an enlargement SF 1.25
c no, because the ratio $\frac{15}{10} \neq$ the ratio $\frac{7.5}{6}$
d yes – this is an enlargement SF 0.2. But this would make the original photograph smaller
e yes – this is an enlargement sf 4.5
f no, because the ratio $\frac{52.5}{15} \neq$ the ratio $\frac{33.5}{10}$
5 a vertices at (2, 4), (6, 4), (6, 6), (4, 6)
b vertices at (−2, 0), (2, 0), (2, 2), (0, 2)
c translation $\begin{pmatrix} -4 \\ -4 \end{pmatrix}$

Ex BG8

1 a diameter **b** tangent **c** segment
d chord **e** arc **f** radius
g sector
2 a 3 cm **b** 1.5 cm
3 a Open compasses to length 4 cm and draw circle
b Open compasses to length 5 cm, place point of compasses at any point P on the circle and draw an arc to cut the circle. Join this point of intersection to point P with a ruler.
4 Open compasses to length 5 cm and draw a circle of radius 5 cm
5 b Construct the perpendicular bisector of AB. Where this cuts AB is the centre O of the circle. Open compasses to length OB, place the point of the compasses on O and draw the circle.
c 2 cm
6 Check constructions. Compasses needed for circle, protractor for constructing sector.
7 Draw a line of length 7 cm and construct its perpendicular bisector to get the mid point O of the line. Open compasses to length 3.5 cm, place point of compasses on O and construct a circle. Open compasses to length 2.5 cm, place point of compasses on O and construct another circle. You will now have 2 concentric circles with a diameter drawn in. Shade as in question.
8 One is an enlargement of the other

Ex BS1

1 Weak negative correlation
Weak positive correlation
No correlation
Strong negative correlation

2 a Division

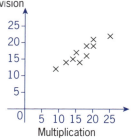

b Strong positive correlation

c Division

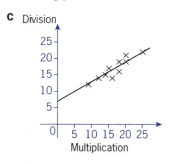

d 21

e This score is outside the range of data plotted – the line of best fit may not be a good predictor for such a low score

3 a

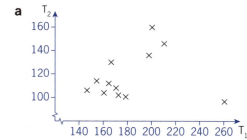

b There is very little evidence of correlation between the T_1 and T_2 times

c There is no suitable line of best fit so cannot estimate the T_2 time

4 a

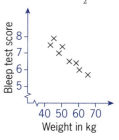

b Strong positive correlation

c

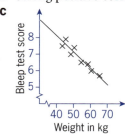

d i 53 kg   **ii** 7.0

Ex BS2

1 a

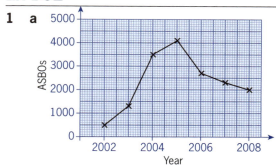

b The number of ASBOs rose sharply from 2002 to a maximum in 2005. They have subsequently fallen to half of the 2005 figure.

2 a Wed 12 pm

b 8 am Friday because the patient's temperature has settled at the normal of 36.9° by then

3 a

(graph of Turnover (£) vs TERM, Spring/Summer 2004–2007)

b The graph shows strong seasonal variation with turnover always being highest in the autumn term and lowest in the summer term. The overall trend in turnover is upward.

4 a

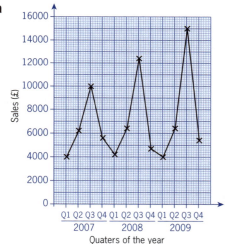

b As would be expected of a beach cafe, the graph shows strong seasonal variation with high sales peaks in the summer quarter. The overall trend in sales is upward.

c Winter 2008 as sales were much lower in Q4 2008 than in the corresponding quarters of 2007 and 2009

Unit C

Ex CN1

1. $\frac{4}{15}$
2. **a** 3 **b** 3.41 **c** 13
   d 17 400 **e** 0.0044 **f** 0.000 0040
3. £6.02
4. $\frac{1}{3}$
5. $3.6 \times 9 = 32.4$
6. **a** 4 days **b** 25 m² **c** $\frac{3}{5}$
7. **a** $\frac{4}{15}$ **b** $\frac{1}{15}$ **c** 3
   d $\frac{19}{20}$ **e** $\frac{11}{12}$ **f** $\frac{5}{9}$
8. He has multiplied the bottom of the fraction by 15 as well as the top. Correct answer is 10
9. **a** 7 complete jars
   b £1.56 (although he will only make a total of 7p profit at this price. Suggest he charges £1.70 per jar to ensure a total profit of over £1)

Ex CN2

1. **a** 0.563 **b** 3.62 **c** 1.07
   d −0.0366 **e** 3.86 **f** 8.39
   g −85.9 **h** 0.829
2. 47.8 cm² (3 sf)
3.

x	−3	−2	−1	0	1
$5x^2 - x$	48	22	6	0	4

4. 7.1 seconds
5. **a** 130.651 **b** $-\frac{5}{6} \approx -0.833$
   c 13.1 (3 sf) **d** 1.496
   e 25.4 cm³ (3 sf)
6.

x	−3	−2	−1	0	1
$2 + 3x^2$	29	14	5	2	5

7. $x = 2$ gives $3x^3 - x = 22$ Too large
   $x = 1.9$ gives $3x^3 - x = 18.677$ Too small
   $x = 1.95$ gives $3x^3 - x = 20.29\ldots$ Too large
   Therefore solution lies between 1.9 and 1.95 and therefore $x = 1.9$ (1 dp)

Ex CN3

1. **a** £6.15 **b** 2.94 km **c** 1.32 kg
   d 8.715 m **e** 1.8 hrs
   f 0.46p (sensibly answer is 0p, i.e. nothing)
2. 168 cm²
3. 37.5%
4. **a** £1564 to nearest £ **b** £1298 to nearest £
5. 12% (2 sf)
6. **a** 6 kg **b** 106 kg (nearest kg)
   c As he puts on weight and passes age 30, the increase per year is likely to level off
7. £6450 (3 sf)
8. **a** £273 000 (3 sf)
   b It is unlikely that house prices will rise by the same percentage for such a long period
9. After 5 years, the bond gives a total of £3286.85 whereas the savings account gives £3250. Obviously, the bond is the better investment if Joan can afford to leave her money untouched for 5 years. If she is likely to need access to some of it within the 5 year period, then she should go for the savings account

Ex CN4

1. 2.45 kg, 2.55 kg
2. The smallest the room could be is 245×455 cm and the largest is 255×465 cm. The carpet is too long.
3. No – Jo may only have jumped 2.15 m
4. **a i** 828.5 m **ii** 828.25 m **iii** 828.005 m
   b part **i**

Ex CN5

1. 25 km
2. No – she has only eaten 1081.25 kcal
3. **a** 287.5 g of butter, 175 g of castor sugar, 5 eggs, 537.5 g plain flour
   b Because the recipe needs exactly 1 egg for every 5 muffins
4. 15 hours

Ex CN6

1. 20 km/hr
2. 105 km
3. 40 mins
4. **a** 19 cm³ (2 sf)
   b £8.81 assuming there is no charge for the manufacture of the bracelet
5. **a** Anyone who sends less than 25 text messages per month
   b Anyone who sends more than 25 text messages per month
6. 2.25 miles
7. Large house £27   Small house £9
8. 80 mins = 1 hr 20 mins
9. **a** 145 cm³ **b** 375 cm³ **c** $1\frac{1}{3}$ mins

Ex CA1

1. **a** (0, 0, 5) **b** (−3, 2, −1) **c** (0, 5, 0)
   d (−3, 4, −2) **e** (3.5, 4, −18)
   f (−2.5, 1.25, 2.5)

Ex CA2

1. **a** 2.6 **b** 1.9 **c** 3.0
   d 3.5 **e** 1.9 **f** −0.2
2. **a** 2.63 **b** 1.86 **c** −1.06
3. **a** Because its length is 1 cm more than its width, hence $(w + 1)$ and its depth is 2 cm more than its width, hence $(w + 2)$. Volume is calculated by multiplying length, width and depth and we know the volume is equal to 100 cm³. This is how we can derive $w(w + 1)(w + 2) = 100$
   b Need to solve $w(w + 1)(w + 2) = 100$
   At $w = 3$, $w(w + 1)(w + 2) = 60$ (smaller than 100) and at $w = 4$, $w(w + 1)(w + 2) = 120$

(larger than 100). Therefore solution lies between $w = 3$ and $w = 4$ i.e. $3 < w < 4$
  c 3.713

Ex CA3

1 a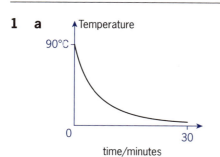

   b

   c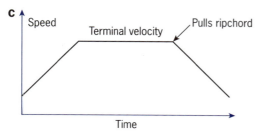

   d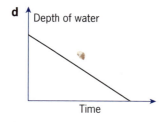

2 a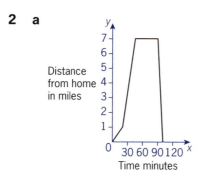

   b 3 mph, 24 mph, 42 mph
   c The gradient is steeper
   d The bus will stop on its way to the pool. The vehicles will not travel at constant speed

Ex CA4

1 a U-shaped parabola with minimum at $(0, -2)$ cutting x-axis at $(-1.4, 0)$ and $(1.4, 0)$
   b U-shaped parabola with minimum at $(0, 3)$
   c U-shaped parabola with minimum at $(0, -5)$ cutting x-axis at $(-2.2, 0)$ and $(2.2, 0)$
   d U-shaped parabola with minimum at $(0, -1)$ cutting x-axis at $(-0.7, 0)$ and $(0.7, 0)$
   e U-shaped parabola with minimum at $(0, -3)$ cutting x-axis at $(-1.2, 0)$ and $(1.2, 0)$
   f U-shaped parabola with minimum at $(0, -7)$ cutting x-axis at $(-3.2, 0)$ and $(3.2, 0)$
   g Dome shaped parabola with maximum at $(0, 10)$ cutting x-axis at $(\pm 3.2, 0)$
   h Dome shaped parabola with maximum at $(0, 2)$ cutting x-axis at $(\pm 1.4, 0)$

2 a ±1.4   b ±2.2   c ±3.2
   d ±0.7   e ±3   f ±1.3
   g ±2   h ±2.2

3 $k < -7$

Ex CG1

1 a Rectangle 12 cm, 8 cm²
   b Triangle 10.6 cm, 5.3 cm²
2 a 30 m²   b 9900 mm²   c 36 m²
3 36 cm²
4 9 units²
5 80 + 35 + 51 = 166 m²
6 a 3 000 000 m²   b 300 hectares
   c £3000

Ex CG2

1 12.6 cm, 12.6 cm²
2 a 25.1 m   50.3 m²   b 128.2 cm   1307.4 cm²
3 a 49.5 m²   b 46.9 m²
4 a 251.3 cm   b 10.1 km
5 a £8.17   b £35.99
6 a 12.5 cm²   b £812.50

Ex CG3

1 A 6 units²   B 2 units²   C 1 unit²
   D 3 units²   E $2\frac{1}{2}$ units²
2 a 6.6 cm²   b 3 cm²
3 Each side will be $\sqrt{56} \approx 7.48$ m
4 5 units²
5 a 9312 m²   b £5504
6 Many answers possible
7 £96.32

Ex CG4

1 a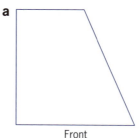
       Front   Side

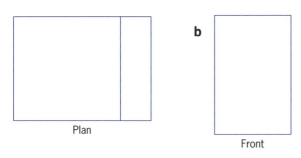

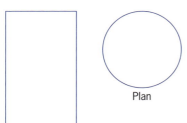

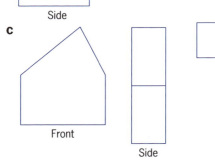

2

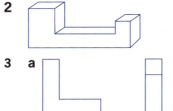

3 a

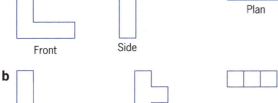

b

4 Various possible nets

Ex CG5

1

	Surface area cm²	Volume cm³
a	92	48
b	246	189
c	422.2	665.9
d	180	108

2 a 640 m³   **b** 640 000 l **c** 88.9 h or 3.7 days
3 Cutting down the dotted line and opening out the curved surface area gives a rectangle whose length is the circumference of the cylinder ($2\pi r$). Therefore area = length × height = $2\pi r × h = 2\pi rh$
4 $V = 1335.2$ cm³ $SA = 691.2$ cm²
5 a 960 cm³   **b** 403.2 g

Ex CG6

1 a 400 mm²   **c** 9000 mm³   **c** 120 cm²
   d 5 000 000 m²   **e** 73 000 cm²
   f 3.2 m³   **g** 435 km²
2 48 units
3 sf 9
4 36 units
5 5 units
6 144 cm²   2304 cm³
7 1 600 000

Ex CS1

1 a Red and yellow as there are equal numbers of these colours
   b $\frac{2}{9}$
2 Sally
3 a i $\frac{3}{8}$ **ii** $\frac{1}{8}$ **iii** 1
   b Need a spinner with 10 sections and 5 sections labelled 1, 3 sections labelled 2, 1 section labelled 3. The 10th section must be labelled with a number not equal to 1, 2 or 3.
4 $\frac{1}{6}$
5 a Because only one of the 6 sections is coloured purple
   b i $\frac{1}{2}$ **ii** $\frac{1}{3}$
6 a 8   **b** 16, 20, 24
7 Bag B because she has a chance of $\frac{1}{2}$ of choosing cherry (in Bag A, her chance is $\frac{4}{9}$ which is less than $\frac{1}{2}$)

Ex CS2

1 a $\frac{2}{5}$ **b** $\frac{11}{15}$
2 0.35
3 a $\frac{4}{9}$ **b** 4
4 a $\frac{1}{2}$ **b** $\frac{1}{5}$ **c** $\frac{7}{10}$
5 a $\frac{7}{8}$ **b** 32
6 a 0.4   **b** 0.2
7 a 3 times as many   **b** 0.12

Ex CS3

1 ABC, ABD, ACD, BCD
2 a

		Peter		
		Red	Purple	Green
Jamal	Purple	PR	PP	PG
	Orange	OR	OP	OG

b $\frac{1}{6}$

3 a

	1	3	5
1	2	4	6
2	3	5	7
4	5	7	9

b i $\frac{1}{9}$ **ii** $\frac{2}{9}$ **iii** $\frac{4}{9}$

Answers 157

4 **a** HH, HT, TH, TT
   b $p(\text{H and a T}) = p(\text{HT or TH}) = \frac{2}{4} = \frac{1}{2}$

5 **a**

White \ Blue	1	2	3	4	5	6
1	2	3	4	5	6	7
2	3	4	5	6	7	8
3	4	5	6	7	8	9
4	5	6	7	8	9	10
5	6	7	8	9	10	11
6	7	8	9	10	11	12

   b 36
   c i 7   ii $\frac{1}{6}$
   d i $\frac{1}{36}$ ii $\frac{1}{9}$ iii $\frac{1}{6}$

6 **a**

Pink \ Blue	1	2	3	4	5	6
1	0	1	2	3	4	5
2	1	0	1	2	3	4
3	2	1	0	1	2	3
4	3	2	1	0	1	2
5	4	3	2	1	0	1
6	5	4	3	2	1	0

   b i 1   ii $\frac{5}{18}$
   c i $\frac{5}{18}$ ii $\frac{2}{9}$ iii $\frac{1}{3}$

7 $\frac{21}{36} = \frac{7}{12}$

Ex CS4

1 No. She is equally likely to get any one of 1, 2, 3, 4, 5, 6 on her next roll
2 No. He is equally likely to get a tail or a head on the next spin

3 **a** Would expect roughly equal frequencies (approx 75) for 1, 2, 3, 4. The high number of 3s suggests the dice is biased
   b $\frac{31}{100}$

4 Red   1 section
   Green   3 sections
   Orange   1 section
   Yellow   1 section
   Blue   4 sections

5 **a** Gary as he has carried out by far the most trials
   b 509
   c Altogether there are 1010 trials, so if coin unbiased would expect approx 505 heads and 505 tails. We have 501 heads and 509 tails which is very close to the expected figures and therefore suggests the coin is unbiased

6 **a**

Score	Frequency
1	3
2	3
3	4
4	3
5	4
6	3
Total	20

   If unbiased, would expect $3\frac{1}{3}$ occurrences of each number, i.e. 3 of some and 4 of others. Results therefore suggest coin unbiased (but based on only 20 trials this conclusion is unreliable)
   b $\frac{1}{5}$

Practice papers

Full answers on enclosed CD-ROM